Cornelia A. P. (Cornelia Atwood Pratt) Comer

A Book of Martyrs

Cornelia A. P. (Cornelia Atwood Pratt) Comer

A Book of Martyrs

ISBN/EAN: 9783743324237

Manufactured in Europe, USA, Canada, Australia, Japa

Cover: Foto ©Lupo / pixelio.de

Manufactured and distributed by brebook publishing software (www.brebook.com)

Cornelia A. P. (Cornelia Atwood Pratt) Comer

A Book of Martyrs

THE IVORY SERIES

Each, 16mo, gilt top, 75 cents

AMOS JUDD. By J. A. Mitchell
    Editor of "Life"

IA. A Love Story. By Q
    [Arthur T. Quiller-Couch]

THE SUICIDE CLUB
    By Robert Louis Stevenson

IRRALIE'S BUSHRANGER
    By E. W. Hornung

A MASTER SPIRIT
    By Harriet Prescott Spofford

MADAME DELPHINE
    By George W. Cable

ONE OF THE VISCONTI
    By Eva Wilder Brodhead

A BOOK OF MARTYRS
    By Cornelia Atwood Pratt

Other Volumes to be announced

A BOOK OF MARTYRS

When first they mixed the Clay of Man and clothed
His Spirit in the Robe of Perfect Beauty,
For Forty Mornings did an evil Cloud
Rain Sorrows over him from Head to Foot;
And when the Forty Mornings passed to Night,
There came one Morning-Shower — one Morning-
   Shower
Of Joy—to Forty of the Rain of Sorrow!
And though the better Fortune came at last
To seal the Work, yet every Wise Man knows
Such Consummation never can be here!

From the Persian of Jàmi.

A BOOK OF MARTYRS

BY

CORNELIA ATWOOD PRATT

CHARLES SCRIBNER'S SONS
NEW YORK, 1896

Copyright, 1896, by
Charles Scribner's Sons

TROW DIRECTORY
PRINTING AND BOOK BINDING COMPANY
NEW YORK

NOTE

OF the stories in this volume, "Witherle's Freedom" and "Serene's Religious Experience" were first published in *The Century Magazine;* "A Consuming Fire," "Hardesty's Cowardice" and "The Honor of a Gentleman" in *Harper's Weekly;* "At the End of the World" in *The Independent.* Thanks are due the publishers of these periodicals for permission to reprint the stories here.

CONTENTS

	PAGE
Witherle's Freedom,	1
Serene's Religious Experience; an Inland Story,	19
An Instance of Chivalry,	45
A Consuming Fire,	71
An Unearned Reward,	89
Hardesty's Cowardice,	111
"The Honor of a Gentleman,"	131
Rivals,	153
At the End of the World,	165

WITHERLE'S FREEDOM

WITHERLE'S FREEDOM

His little world was blankly astonished when Witherle dropped out of it. His disappearance was as his life had been, neat, methodical, well-arranged; but why did he go at all?

He had lived through thirty-seven years of a discreetly conducted existence with apparent satisfaction; he had been in the ministry for fifteen years; he had been married nearly as long; he was in no sort of difficulty, theological, financial, or marital; he possessed the favor of his superiors in the church, the confidence of his wife, and he had recently come into a small fortune bequeathed him by a great-aunt. Every one regarded him as very "comfortably fixed" —for a minister.

Of all the above-enumerated blessings he had divested himself methodically, as a man folds up and lays aside worn garments. He resigned his charge, he transferred his property to his wife, and wrote her a farewell note in which he said, in a light-hearted way which she mistook for incoherence, that she would never see him again. These things done, he dropped out of the sight of men as completely as a stone fallen into a pond.

His friends speculated and investigated, curiously, eagerly, fearfully, but to no purpose. What was the motive? Where had he gone? Had he committed suicide? Was he insane? The elders of the church employed a detective, and the friends of his wife took up the search, but Witherle was not found. He had left as little trace whereby he could be followed as a meteor leaves when it rushes across the sky.

Presently, of course, interest in the event subsided; the church got a new minister; Witherle's wife went back to her own people; the world appeared to forget. But there was a man of Witherle's congregation named Lowndes who still meditated the unsolved problem at odd moments. He was a practical man of affairs, with the psychological instinct, and he found the question of why people do the things that they do perennially interesting. Humanity from any point of view is a touching spectacle; from a business standpoint it is infinitely droll. Personally Lowndes was one of the wholesome natures for whom there are more certainties than uncertainties in life, and he felt for Witherle the protecting friendliness that a strong man sometimes has for one less strong. He advised him as to his investments on week-days, and listened patiently Sunday after Sunday, as the lesser man expounded the mysteries of creation and the ways of the Creator, sustained by the reflection that Witherle was better than his sermons. He did not consider him an interesting man, but he believed him to be a good one. When Witherle was no longer at hand, Lowndes counselled and planned for his wife, and otherwise made himself as useful as the circumstances would permit. He felt sorry for Witherle's wife, a nervous woman to whom had come as sharp an upheaval of life as death itself could have brought about, without the comfort of the reflection that the Lord had taken away.

Fate, who sometimes delivers the ball to those who are ready to play, decreed that, in May, about a year after Witherle's disappearance, Lowndes should be summoned from the Pennsylvania village where he lived to one of the cities of an adjoining State. His business took him along the dingy riverfront of the town. Crossing a bridge one evening toward sunset, he stopped idly to note the shifting iridescent tints that converted the river for the hour into a heavenly water-way between the two purgatorial banks lined with warehouses and elevators black with the inexpressibly mussy and depressing blackness of the soot of soft coal. His glance fell upon a coal-barge being loaded at the nearest wharf. He leaned over the rail, wondering why the lines of the figure of one of the workmen looked familiar to him. The man seemed to be shovelling coal with a peculiar zest. As this is a species of toil not usually performed for the love of it, his manner naturally attracted attention. While Lowndes still stood there pondering the problematical familiarity of his back, the man turned. Lowndes clutched the rail. "By Jove!" he said, excitedly, for he saw that the features were the features of Witherle. Their expression was exultant and illuminated beyond anything ever vouchsafed to that plodding gospeller. Moving along the bridge to a point just above the barge, he took out his watch and looked at it. It was nearly six o'clock.

The next fifteen minutes were exciting ones for Lowndes. His mind was in a tumult. It is no light matter to make one's self the arbiter of another man's destiny; and he knew enough of Witherle to feel sure that the man's future was in his hands. He looked down at him dubiously, his strong hands still clutching the rail tensely. For a minute he felt that he must move on without making his presence known, but even as he resolved, the clocks and whistles clamorously announced the hour.

When the men quitted their work, the man whom Lowndes's eyes were following came up the stairs that led to the bridge. As he passed, Lowndes laid a hand lightly on his shoulder.

"How are you, Witherle?" he said.

The man stared at him blankly a second, recoiled, and his face turned livid as he shook off the friendly hand. The other men had passed on, and they were alone on the bridge.

"I'm a free man," said Witherle, loudly, throwing back his shoulders. "Before God, I'm a free man for the first time in my life.. What do you want with me?"

"Don't rave," said Lowndes, sharply. "I sha'n't hurt you. You couldn't expect me to pass you without speaking, could you?"

"Then you weren't looking for me?" asked Witherle, abjectly.

"I have business on hand." Lowndes spoke impatiently, for he did not enjoy seeing his old friend cower. "I am here for the Diamond Oil Co. I was crossing the bridge just now, when I saw a man down there shovelling coal as if he liked it; and I delayed to look, and saw it was you. So I waited for you. That is all there is of it. You needn't stop if you don't wish."

Witherle drew a deep breath. "My nerves aren't what they were," he said, apologetically. "It played the mischief with them to—" He left the sentence hanging in the air.

"If you weren't going to like the results, you needn't have gone," observed Lowndes, in an impartial tone. "Nobody has been exactly able to see the reasons for your departure. You left the folks at home a good deal stirred up."

"What do they say about me there?"

Lowndes hesitated. "Most of them say you were crazy. Your wife has gone back to her people."

"Ah!"

Lowndes looked at the man with a sudden impulse of pity. He was leaning against the rail, breathing heavily. His face was white beneath the soot, but in his eyes still flamed that incomprehensible ecstasy. He was inebriate with the subtle stimulus of some transcendent thought. But what thought? And what had brought him here? This creature, with his sensitive mouth, his idealist's eyes, his scholar's hands, black and hardened now but still clearly recognizable, was at least more out of place among the coal-heavers than he had been in the pulpit. Lowndes felt mightily upon him the desire to shepherd this man back to some more sheltered fold. The highways of existence were not for his feet; not for his lips the "Song of the Open Road." He did not resist the desire to say, meditatively:

"You have no children——"

"God in His mercy be praised for that one blessing!" Witherle muttered. But Lowndes went on as if he did not hear:

"But you might think of your wife."

"I have thought of her — too much. I thought about everything too much. I am tired of thinking," said Witherle. "I wonder if you understand?"

"Not in the least."

Witherle looked about him restlessly. "Come where we can talk—down there on that pile of boards. I think I'd like to talk. It is very simple when once you understand it."

He led the way to the opposite end of the bridge, and down an embankment to a lumber-pile at the water's edge. Up the river the May sun had gone down in splendor, leaving the water crimson-stained. Witherle sat down where he could look along the river-reaches.

"Hold on a minute, Witherle. Don't talk to me unless you are sure you want to."

"That's all right. There's nothing much to tell. I don't seem to mind your understanding."

Witherle was silent a minute.

"It is very simple," he said again. "This is the way I think about it. Either you do the things you want to do in this world or else you don't. I had never done what I wanted until I left home. I didn't mean to hurt anybody by coming away in that style, and I don't think that I did. I'd rather not be selfish, but life got so dull. I couldn't stand it. I had to have a change. I had to come. The things you have to do you do. There was a Frenchman once who committed suicide and left a note that said: 'Tired of this eternal buttoning and unbuttoning.' I know how he felt. I don't know how other men manage to live. Perhaps their work means more to them than mine had come to mean to me. It was just dull, that was all, and I had to come."

Lowndes stared. Truly it was delightfully simple. "Why, man, you can't chuck your responsibilities overboard like that. Your wife——"

"When I was twenty-one," interrupted Witherle, "I was in love. The girl married somebody else. Before I met my wife she had cared for a man who married another woman. You see how it was. We were going to save the pieces together. As a business arrangement that sort of thing is all right. I haven't a word to say against it. She is a good woman, and we got on as well as most people, only life was not ecstasy to either of us. Can't you see us tied together, snaking our way along through existence as if it were some gray desert, and we crawling on and on over the sand, always with our faces bent to it, and nothing showing itself in our way but the white bones of the men and women who had travelled along there before us — grinning skulls mostly? Can't you see it?"

Looking up, he caught an expression in Lowndes's eyes the meaning of which he suspected. "Oh, you needn't be afraid," he added, hastily, "that this is insanity. It's only imagination. That's the way I felt. And my work was only another long desert to be toiled through—with the Sphinx at the end. I wasn't a successful preacher, and you know it. I hadn't any grip on men. I hadn't any grip on myself—or God. I couldn't see any use or any meaning or any joy in it. The whole thing choked me. I wanted a simpler, more elemental life. I wanted to go up and down the earth and try new forms of living, new ways of doing things, new people. Life—that was what I wanted; to feel the pulse of the world throb under my touch, to be in the stir, to be doing something. I was always haunted by the conviction that life was tremendous if only you once got at it. I couldn't get at it where I was. I was rotting away. So when that money was left me it came like a godsend. I knew my wife could live on that, and I didn't think she'd miss me much, so I just came off."

"And you like it?"

The man's eyes flamed. "Like it? It's great! It's the only thing there is. I've been from Maine to California this year. I wintered in a Michigan lumber-camp—that was hell. I was a boat-hand on the Columbia last summer—that was heaven. I worked in a coal-mine two months—a scab workman, you understand. And now I'm at this. I tell you, it is fine to get rid of cudgelling your brains for ideas that aren't there, and of pretending to teach people something you don't know, and take to working with your hands nine hours a day and sleeping like a log all night. I hadn't slept for months, you know. These people tell me about themselves. I'm seeing what life is like. I'm getting down to the foundations. I've learned more about humanity in the last six months than I ever knew in all my life. I believe I've learned more about religion. I'm getting hold of things.

It's like getting out on the open sea after that desert I was talking about—don't you see? And it all tastes so good to me!" He dropped his head into his hands, exhausted by the flood of words he had poured rapidly out.

Lowndes hesitated long before he spoke. He was reflecting that Witherle's exaltation was pathological—he was drunk with the air of the open road.

"Poor little devil!" he thought. "One might let alone a man who finds ecstasy in being a coal-heaver; but it won't do."

"Life is big," he admitted, slowly; "it's tremendous, if you like; it's all you say—but it isn't for you. Don't you see it is too late? We're all of us under bonds to keep the world's peace and finish the contracts we undertake. You're out of bounds now. You have got to come back."

Witherle stared at him blankly. "You say that? After what I've told you? Why, there's nothing to go back for. And here—there is everything! What harm am I doing, I'd like to know? Who is hurt? What claims has that life on me? Confound you!" his wrath rising fiercely, "how dare you talk like that to me? Why isn't life for me as well as for you?"

This Witherle was a man he did not know. Lowndes felt a little heart-sick, but only the more convinced that he must make his point.

"If you didn't feel that you were out of bounds, why were you afraid of me when I came along?"

The thrust told. Witherle was silent. Lowndes went on: "Bread isn't as interesting as champagne, I know, but there is more in it, in the long run. However, that's neither here nor there—if a man has a right to his champagne. But you haven't. You are mistaken about your wife. She was all broken up. I don't pretend to say she was desperately fond of you. I don't know anything about that. But, anyhow, she had made for herself a kind of life of which you were the centre, and it was all the life she had. You had no right to break it to pieces getting what you wanted. That's a brutal thing for a man to do. She looked very miserable, when I saw her. You've got to go back."

Witherle turned his head from side to side restlessly, as a sick man turns on the pillow.

"How can I go back?" he cried, keenly protesting. "Don't you see it's impossible? I've burned my ships."

"That's easy enough. You went off in a fit of double consciousness, or temporary insanity, or something like that, and I found you down here. It will be easy enough to reinstate you. I'll see to that."

"That would be a lie," said Witherle, resolutely.

Lowndes stared at him curiously, reflecting upon the fastidiousness with which men pick and choose their offenses against righteousness, embracing one joyously and rejecting another with scorn.

"Yes; so it would. But I have offered to do the lying for you, and you *are* off your head, you know."

"How?" demanded Witherle, sharply.

"Any man is off his head who can't take life as it comes, the bad and the good, and bear up under it. Suicide is insanity. You tried to commit suicide in the cowardliest way, by getting rid of your responsibilities and saving your worthless breath. Old man, it won't do. You say you've learned something about religion and humanity—come back and tell us about it."

Witherle listened to his sentence in silence. His long lower lip trembled.

"Anything more?" he demanded.

"That's all. It won't do."

The man dropped his head into his hands and sat absolutely still. Lowndes watched the river growing grayer and grayer, and listened to the lapping of the water against the lumber, remembering that one of the poets had said it was a risky business tampering with souls, and matter enough to save one's own. The reflection made him feel a little faint. What if Witherle had a right to that life in spite of everything—that life for which he had given all?

Witherle lifted his head at last. "You are sure my wife was broken up over it?" he demanded, despairingly.

"Sure."

Witherle cast one longing glance across the darkening river to the black outlines of the barge. There, ah, even there, the breath of life was sweet upon his lips, and toil was good, and existence was worth while.

"I thought no soul in the world had a claim on me. Curse duty! The life of a rat in a cage!" he cried. "Oh, Lord, I haven't the head nor the heart for it!"

The words were bitter, but his voice broke with compliance. He rose to his feet and stretched out his arms with a fierce gesture, then dropped them heavily by his side.

"Come on," he said.

Lowndes, watching him with that curious, heart-sickening sympathy growing upon him, was aware that he had seen the end of a soul's revolt. Rightly or wrongly, Witherle's freedom was over.

SERENE'S RELIGIOUS EXPERIENCE;
AN INLAND STORY

SERENE'S RELIGIOUS EXPERIENCE; AN INLAND STORY

SERENE and young Jessup, the schoolteacher, were leaning over the front gate together in the warm summer dusk.

"See them sparkin' out there?" inquired Serene's father, standing at the door with his hands in his pockets, and peering out speculatively.

"Now, father, when you know that ain't Serene's line."

It was Mrs. Sayles who spoke. Perhaps there was the echo of a faint regret in her voice, for she wished to see her daughter "respectit like the lave"; but "sparkin'" had never been Serene's line.

"Serene wouldn't know how," said her big brother.

"There's other things that's a worse waste o' time," observed Mr. Sayles, meditatively, "and one on 'em's 'Doniram Jessup's everlastin' talk-talk-talkin' to no puppus. He's none so smart if he does teach school. He'd do better on the farm with his father."

"He's more'n three hundred dollars ahead, and goin' to strike out for himself, he says," observed the big brother, admiringly.

"Huh! My son, I've seen smart young men strike out for themselves 'fore ever you was born, and I've seen their fathers swim out after 'em—and sink," said Mr. Sayles, oracularly.

Outside the June twilight was deepening, but Serene and the school-teacher still leaned tranquilly over the picket-gate. The fragrance of the lemon-lilies that grew along the fence was in the air, and over Serene's left shoulder, if she had turned to look, she would have seen the slight yellow crescent of the new moon sliding down behind the trees.

They were talking eagerly, but it was only about what he had written in regard to "Theory and Practice" at the last county examination.

"I think you carry out your ideas real well," Serene said, admiringly, when he had finished his exposition. "'Tisn't everybody does that. I know I've learned a good deal more this term than I ever thought to when I started in."

The teacher was visibly pleased. He was a slight, wiry little fellow, with alert eyes, a cynical smile, and an expression of self-confidence, which was justifiable only on the supposition that he had valuable information as to his talents and capacity unknown to the world at large.

"I think you *have* learned a good deal of me," he observed, condescendingly; "more than any of the younger ones. I have taken some pains with you. It's a pleasure to teach willing learners."

At this morsel of praise, expressed in such a strikingly original manner, Serene flushed and looked prettier than ever. She was always pretty, this slip of a girl, with olive skin, pink cheeks, and big, dark eyes, and she always looked a little too decorative, too fanciful, for her environment in this substantial brick farm-house, set in the midst of fat, level acres of good Ohio land. It was as if a Dresden china shepherdess had been put upon their kitchen mantel-shelf.

Don Jessup stooped and picked a cluster of the pink wild rosebuds, whose bushes were scattered along the road outside the fence, and handed them to her with an admiring look. Why, he scarcely knew; it is as involuntary and natural a thing for any one to pay passing tribute to a pretty girl as for the summer wind to kiss the clover. Serene read the momentary impulse better than he did himself, and took the buds with deepening color and a beating heart.

"He gives them to me because he thinks I look like that," she thought with a quick, happy thrill.

"Yes," he went on, rather confusedly, his mind being divided between what he was saying and a curiosity to find out if she would be as angry as she was the last time if he should try to kiss the nearest pink cheek; "I think it would be a good idea for you to keep on with your algebra by yourself, and you might read that history you began. I don't know who's going to have the school next fall. Now, if I were going to be here this summer, I——"

"Why, Don," Serene interrupted him, using the name she had not often spoken since Adoniram Jessup, after a couple of years in the High School, had come back to live at home, and to teach in their district—"why, Don, I thought your mother said you were going to help on the farm this summer."

Adoniram smiled, a thin-lipped, complacent little smile.

"Father did talk that some, but I've decided to go West—and I start to-morrow."

To-morrow! And that great, hungry West, which swallows up people so remorselessly! Something ailed Serene's heart; she hoped he could not hear it beating, and she waited a minute before saying, quietly:

"Isn't this sort of sudden?"

"I don't like to air my plans too much. There's many a slip, you know."

"You'll want to come to the house and say good-by to the folks, and tell us all about it?" As he nodded assent, she turned and preceded him up the narrow path.

"When will you be back?" she asked over her shoulder.

"Maybe never. If I have any luck, I'd like the old people to come out to me. I'm not leaving anything else here."

"You needn't have told *me* so," said Serene to herself.

"Father, boys, here's Don come in to say good-by. He's going West to-morrow."

"Well, 'Doniram Jessup! Why don't you give us a s'prise party and be done with it?"

Don smiled cheerfully at this tribute to his secretive powers, and sitting down on the edge of the porch, began to explain.

Serene glanced around to see that all were listening, and then slipped quietly out through the kitchen to the high back porch, where she found a seat behind the new patent "creamery," and leaning her head against it, indulged in the luxury of a few dry sobs. Tears she dared not shed, for tears leave traces. Though "sparkin'" had not been Serene's line, love may come to any human creature, and little Serene had learned more that spring than the teacher had meant to impart or she to acquire.

When the five minutes she had allotted to her grief were past she went back to the group at the front of the house as unnoticed as she had left them. Her father was chaffing Jessup good-naturedly on his need of more room to grow in, and Don was responding with placid ease. It was not chaff, indeed, that could disturb his convictions as to his personal importance to the development of the great West. Presently he rose and shook hands with them all, including herself—for whom he had no special word—said a general good-by, and left them.

"He's thinking of himself," thought Serene a little bitterly, as she watched him go down the yard; "he is so full of his plans and his future he hardly knows I am here. I don't believe he ever knew it!"

To most people the loss of the possible affection of Don Jessup would not have seemed a heavy one, but the human heart is an incomprehensible thing, and the next six weeks were hard for Serene. For the first time in her life she realized how much we can want that which we may not have, and she rebelled against the knowledge.

"Why?" she asked herself, and "why?" Why should she have cared, since he, it seemed, did not? Why couldn't she stop caring now? And, oh, why had he been so dangerously kind when he did not care? Poor little Serene! she did not know that we involuntarily feel a tenderness almost as exquisite as that of love itself toward whatever feeds the fountain of our vanity.

Presently, tired of asking herself, she turned to asking Heaven, which is easier. For we cannot comfortably blame ourselves for the inability to answer our own inconvenient inquiries, but Heaven we can both ask and blame. Serene had never troubled

Heaven much before, but now, in desperation, she battered at its portals night and day. She did not pray, you understand, to be given the love which many small signs had taught her to believe might be hers, the love that, nevertheless, had not come near to her. Though young, she was reasonable. She instinctively recognized that when we cannot be happy it is necessary for us to be comfortable, if we are still to live. So, after a week or two of rebellion, she asked for peace, sure that if it existed for her anywhere in the universe, God held it in His keeping, for, now, no mortal did.

She prayed as she went about her work by day; she prayed as she knelt by her window at evening, looking out on the starlit world; she prayed when she woke late in the night and found her room full of the desolate white light of the waning moon, and always the same prayer.

"Lord," said Serene, "this is a little thing that I am going through. Make me feel that it is a little thing. Make me stop caring. But if you *can't*, then show me that you care that I am not happy. If I could feel you knew and cared, I think I might be happier."

But in her heart she felt no answer, and peace did not come to fill the place of happiness.

In our most miserable hours fantastic troubles and apprehensions of the impossible often come to heap themselves upon our real griefs, making up a load which is heavier than we can bear. Serene began to wonder if God heard—if He was there at all.

Her people noticed that she grew thin and tired-looking, and attributed it to the fierce hot weather. For it was the strange summer long remembered in the inland country where they lived as the season of the great drought. There had been a heavy snowfall late in April; from that time till late in August no rain fell. The heat was terrible. Dust was everywhere. The passage of time from one scorching week to another was measured by the thickening of its heavy inches on the highway; it rose in clouds about the feet of cattle in the burnt-up clover-fields. The roadside grass turned to tinder, and where a careless match had been dropped, or the ashes shaken from a pipe, there were long, black stretches of seared ground to tell the tale. The resurrection of the dead seemed no greater miracle than these blackened fields should shortly turn to living green again, under the quiet influence of autumn rains.

And now, in the early days of August, when the skies were brass, the sun a tongue of flame, and the yellow dust pervaded the air like an ever-thickening fog, a strange story came creeping up from the country south of them. "Down in Paulding," where much of the land still lay under the primeval forest, and solitary sawmills were the advance-guards of civilization; where there were great marshes, deep woods, and one impenetrable tamarack swamp, seemed the proper place for such a thing to happen if it were to happen at all. The story was of a farmer who went out one Sunday morning to look at his corn-field, forty good acres of newly cleared land, ploughed this year only for the second time. The stunted stalks quivered in the hot air, panting for water; the blades were drooping and wilted like the leaves of a plant torn up from the ground. He looked from his blasted crop to the pitiless skies, and, lifting a menacing hand, cursed Heaven because of it. Those who told the story quoted the words he used, with voices awkwardly lowered; but there was nothing impressive in his vulgar, insensate defiance. He was merely swearing a shade more imaginatively than was his wont. The impressive thing was that, as he stood with upraised hand and cursing lips, he was suddenly stricken with paralysis, and stood rooted to the spot, holding up the threatening arm, which was never to be lowered. This was the first story. They heard stranger things afterward: that his family were unable to remove him from the spot; that he was burning with an inward fire which did not consume, and no man dared to lay hand on him, or even approach him, because of the heat of his body.

It was said that this was clearly a judgment, and it was much talked of and wondered over. Serene listened to these stories with a singular exultation, and devoutly trusted that they were true. She had needed a visible miracle, and here was one to her hand. Why should not such things happen now as well as in Bible days? And if the Lord descended in justice, why not in mercy? The thing she hungered for was to know that He kept in touch with each individual human life, that He listened, that He cared. If He heard the voice of blasphemy,

then surely He was not deaf to that of praise
—or agony. She said to herself, feverishly,
"I must know, I must see for myself, if it is
true."

She said to her father: "Don't you think
I might go down to Aunt Mari's in Paulding
for a week? It does seem as if it might be
cooler down there in the woods," and her
tired face attested her need of change and
rest. He looked at her with kindly eyes.

"Don't s'pose it will do you no great
harm, if your mother'll manage without you;
but your Aunt Mari's house ain't as cool as
this one, Serene."

"It's different, anyhow," said the girl,
and went away to write a postal-card to
Aunt Mari and to pack her valise.

When she set out, in a day or two, it was
with as high a hope as ever French peasant
maid took on pilgrimage to Loretto. She
hoped to be cured of all her spiritual ills, but
how, she hardly knew. The trip was one
they often made with horses, but Serene,
going alone, took the new railroad that ran
southward into the heart of the forests and
the swamps. Her cousin Dan, with his colt
and road-cart, met her at the clearing, where
a shed beside a water-tank did duty for town

and station, and drove her home. Her Aunt Mari was getting dinner, and, after removing her hat, Serene went out to the kitchen, and sat down on the settee. The day was stifling, and the kitchen was over-heated, but Aunt Mari was standing over the stove frying ham with unimpaired serenity.

"Well, and so you thought it would be cooler down here, Serene? I'm real glad to see you, but I can't promise much of nothin' about the weather. We've suffered as much as most down here."

Serene saw her opportunity.

"We heard your corn was worse than it is with us. What was there in that story, Aunt Mari, about the man who was paralyzed on a Sunday morning?"

"Par'lyzed, child? I don't know as I just know what you mean."

"But he lived real near here," persisted Serene—"two miles south and three east of the station, they said. That would be just south of here. And we've heard a good deal about it. You must know, Aunt Mari."

"Must be old man Burley's sunstroke. That's the only thing that's happened, and there was some talk about that. He's a

Dunkard, you know, and they are mightily set on their church. Week ago Sunday was their day for love-feast, and it was a hundred an' seven in the shade. He hadn't been feelin' well, and his wife she just begged him not to go out; but he said he guessed the Lord couldn't make any weather too hot for him to go to church in. So he just hitched up and started, but he got a sunstroke before he was half-way there, and they had to turn round and bring him home again. He come to all right, but he ain't well yet. Some folks thinks what he said 'bout the weather was pretty presumpshus, but I dunno. Seems if he might use some freedom of speech with the Lord if anybody could, for he's been a profitable servant. A good man has some rights. I don't hold with gossipin' 'bout such things, and callin' on 'em 'visitations' when they happen to better folks than me—why, Serene! what's the matter?" in a shrill crescendo of alarm, for the heat, the journey, and the disappointment had been too much for the girl. Her head swam as she grasped the gist of her aunt's story, and perceived that upon this simple foundation must have been built the lurid tale which had drawn her here, and for the first time in her healthy, unemotional life she quietly fainted away.

When she came to herself she was lying on the bed in Aunt Mari's spare room. The spare room was under the western eaves, and there were feathers on the bed. Up the stairway from the kitchen floated the pervasive odor of frying ham. A circle of anxious people, whose presence made the stuffy room still stuffier, were eagerly watching her. Opening her languid eyes to these material discomforts of her situation, she closed them again. She felt very ill, and the only thing in her mind was the conviction that had overtaken her just as she fainted—"Then God is no nearer in Paulding than at home."

As the result of closing her eyes seemed to be the deluging of her face with water until she choked, she decided to reopen them.

"Well," said Aunt Mari, heartily, "that looks more like. How do you feel, Serene? Wasn't it singular that you should go off so, just when I was tellin' you 'bout 'Lishe Burley's sunstroke? I declare, I was frightened when I looked around and saw you. Your uncle would bring you up here and put you on the bed, though I told him 't was cooler in the settin'-room. But he seemed to think this was the thing to do."

"I wish he'd take me down again," said Serene, feebly and ungratefully, "and" (after deliberation) "put me in the spring-house."

"What you need is somethin' to eat," said Aunt Mari with decision. "I'll make you a cup of hot tea, and" (not heeding the gesture of dissent) "I don't believe that ham's cold yet."

Serene had come to stay a week, and a week accordingly she stayed. The days were very long and very hot; the nights on the feather-bed under the eaves still longer and hotter. She had very little to say for herself, and thought still less. There is a form of despair which amounts to coma.

"Serene's never what you might call sprightly," observed Aunt Mari in confidence to Uncle Dan'el, "but this time, seems if—well, I s'pose it's the weather. Wonder if I'll ever see any weather on this earth to make me stop talkin'?" It was a relief all around when the day came for her departure.

"I'll do better next time, Aunt Mari," said Serene as she stepped aboard the train;

but she did not greatly care that she had not done well this time.

When the short journey was half over, the train made a longer stop than usual at one of the way stations. Then, after some talking, the passengers gradually left the car. Serene noticed these things vaguely, but paid no attention to their meaning. Presently a friendly brakeman approached and touched her on the shoulder.

"Didn't you hear 'em say, Miss, there was a freight wreck ahead, and we can't go on till the track is clear?"

"How long will it be?" asked Serene, slowly finding the way out of her reverie.

"Mebbe two hours now, and mebbe longer. I'll carry your bag into the depot, if you like," and he possessed himself of the shiny black valise seamed with grayish cracks, and led the way out of the car.

The station at Arkswheel is a small and grimy structure set down on a cinder bank. Across the street on one corner is a foundry, and opposite that a stave-factory with a lumber-yard about it. In the shadow of the piled-up staves, like a lily among thorns, stands a Gothic chapel, small, but architecturally good. Serene, looking out of the dusty window, saw it, and wondered that a church should be planted in such a place. When, presently, although it was a week-day, the bell began to ring, she turned to a woman sitting next to her for an explanation.

"That's the church Mr. Bellington built. He owns the foundry here. They have meeting there 'most any time. 'Piscopal, it is."

"I don't know much about that denomination," observed Serene, sedately.

"My husband's sister-in-law that I visit here goes there. She says her minister just does take the cake. They think the world an' all of him."

Serene no longer looked interested. The woman rose, and walked about the room, examining the maps and time-tables. By and by she came back and stopped beside Serene.

"If we've got to wait till nobody knows when, we might just as well go over there and see what's goin' on—to the church, I mean. Mebbe 't would pass the time."

Inside the little church the light was so subdued that it almost produced the grateful effect of coolness. As they sat down behind the small and scattered congregation, Serene felt that it was a place to rest. The service, which she had never heard before, affected her like music that she did not understand. The rector was a young man with a heavily lined face. His eyes were dark and troubled, his voice sweet and penetrating. When he began his sermon she became suddenly aware that she was hearing some one to whom what he discerned of spiritual truth was the overwhelmingly important thing in life, and she listened eagerly. This was St. Bartholomew's day, it appeared. Serene did not remember very clearly who he was, but she understood this preacher when, dropping his notes and leaning over his desk, he seemed to be scrutinizing each individual face in the audience before him to find one responsive to his words.

He was not minded, he said, to talk to them of any lesson to be drawn from the life of St. Bartholomew, of whom so little was known save that he lived in and suffered for the faith. The one thought that he had to give had occurred to him in connection with that bloody night's work in France so long ago, of which this was the anniversary, when thousands were put to death because of their faith.

"Such things do not happen nowadays," he went on. "That form of persecution is over. Instead of it, we have seen the dawning of what may be a darker day, when those who profess the faith of Christ have themselves turned to persecute the faith which is in their hearts. Faith—the word means to me that trust in God's plans for us which brings confidence to the soul even when we stand in horrible fear of life, and mental peace even when we are facing that which we cannot understand. We persecute our faith in many ingenious ways, but perhaps those torture themselves most whose religion is most emotional—those who are only sure that God is with them when they feel the peace of His presence in their hearts. A great divine said long ago that to love God thus is to love Him for the spiritual loaves and fishes, which He does not mean always to be our food. But for those who think that He is not with them when they are unaware of His presence so, I have this word: When you cannot find God in your hearts, then turn and look for Him in your lives. When you are soul-sick, discouraged, unhappy; when you feel neither joy nor peace, nor even the comfort of a dull satisfaction in earth; when life is nothing to you, and you wish for death, then ask yourself, What does God mean by this? For there is surely some lesson for you in that pain which you must learn before you leave it. You are not so young as to believe that you were meant for happiness. You know that you were made for discipline. And the discipline of life is the learning of the things *God wishes us to know*, even in hardest ways. But He is in the things we must learn, and in the ways we learn them. There is a marginal reading of the first chapter of the revised version of the Gospel of St. John which conveys my meaning: 'That which hath been made was life in Him, and the life [or, as some commentators read, and I prefer it, simply *life*] was the light of men.' That is, before Christ's coming the light of men was in the experience to be gained in the lives He gave them. And it is still true. Not His life only, then, but your life and mine, which we know to the bitter-sweet depths, and whose lessons grow clearer and clearer before us, are to guide us. Life *is* the light of men. I sometimes think that this, and this only, is rejecting Christ — to refuse to find Him in the life He gives us."

Serene heard no more. What else was

said she did not know. She had seized upon his words, and was applying them to her own experiences with a fast-beating heart, to see if haply she had learned anything by them that "God wanted her to know." She had loved unselfishly. Was not that something? She had learned that despair and distrust are not the attitudes in which loss may be safely met. She had become conscious in a blind way that the world was larger and nearer to her than it used to be, and she was coming to feel a sense of community in all human suffering. Were not all these good things?

When the congregation knelt for the last prayer, Serene knelt with them, but did not rise again. She did not respond even when her companion touched her on the shoulder before turning to go. She could not lift her face just then, full as it was of that strange rapture which came of the sudden clear realization that her life was the tool in the hands of the Infinite by which her soul was shaped. "Let me be chastened forever," the heart cries in such a moment, "so that I but learn more of thy ways!"

Some one came slowly down the aisle at last, and stopped, hesitating, beside the pew where she still knelt. Serene looked up. It was the rector. He saw a slender girl in unbecoming dress, whose wild-rose face was quivering with excitement. She saw a man, not old, whose thin features nevertheless wore the look of one who has faced life for a long time dauntlessly—the face of a good fighter.

"Oh, sir, is it true what you said?" she demanded, breathlessly.

"It is what I live upon," he answered, "the belief that it is true." And then, because he saw that she had no further need of him, he passed on, and left her in the little church alone. When at length she recrossed the street to the station, the train was ready, and in another hour she was at home.

They were glad to see her at home, and they had a great deal to tell that had happened to them in the week. They wondered a little that she did not relate more concerning her journey, but they were used to Serene's silences, and her mother was satisfied with the effect of the visit when she observed that Serene seemed to take pleasure in everything she did, even in the washing of the supper-dishes.

There were threatening clouds in the sky

that evening, as there had often been before that summer, but people were weary of saying that it looked like a shower. Nevertheless, when Serene woke in the night, not only was there vivid lightning in the sky, and the roll of distant but approaching thunder, but there was also the unfamiliar sound of rain blown sharply against the roof, and a delicious coolness in the room. The long drought was broken.

She sat up in her white bed to hear the joyous sound more clearly. It was as though the thunder said, "Lift up your heart!" And the rapturous throbbing of the rain seemed like the gracious downpouring of a needed shower on her own parched and thirsty life.

AN INSTANCE OF CHIVALRY

AN INSTANCE OF CHIVALRY

APPLEGATE entered his door that night with a delightful sense of the difference between the sharp November air without and the warmth and brightness within, but as he stood in the little square hall taking off his overcoat, this comfortable feeling gave way to a heart-sick shrinking of which he was unashamed. He was a man of peace, and through the closed door of the sitting-room came the sound of voluble and angry speech. The voice was that of Mrs. Applegate.

Reluctantly he pushed open the door. It was a pretty quarrel as it stood. At one end of the little room, gay with light and color, was Julie, leaning on the mantel. She wore a crimson house-dress a trifle low at the throat, which set off vividly her rich, dark beauty. Undoubtedly she had beauty, and a singular, gypsy-like piquancy as well. It did not seem to matter that the gown was slightly shabby. She was kicking the white fur hearth-rug petulantly now and then to punctuate her remarks.

Dora, with her book in her lap, sat in a low chair by the lamp. Dora was a slender, self-possessed girl of fifteen, in whose cold, young eyes her step-mother had read from the first a concentrated and silent disapproval which was really very exasperating.

"It's the first time that woman has set foot in this house since I've been the mistress of it," Julie was saying, angrily. "Maybe she thinks I ain't fine enough for her to call on. Lord! I'd like to tell her what I think of her. It was her business to ask for me, and it was your business to call me, whether she did or not. Maybe you think I ain't enough of a lady to answer Mrs. Buel Parry's questions. I'd like to have you remember I'm your father's wife!"

Dora's head dropped lower in an agony of vicarious shame. How, her severe young mind was asking itself, could any woman bear to give herself away to such an appalling extent? To reveal that one had thwarted social ambitions; to admit that one might not seem a lady—degradation could go no farther in the young girl's eyes.

"What's the matter, Dora?" asked Applegate, quietly, in the lull following Julie's last remark.

"Mrs. Parry came to the door to ask what sort of a servant Mary Samphill had been. Mamma was in the kitchen, teaching the new girl how to mould bread, and I answered Mrs. Parry's questions. She did not ask for any one."

"I say it was Dora's business to ask her in and call me. Whose servant was Mary Samphill, I'd like to know. Was she Dora's?"

Applegate crossed the room to the open fire and stretched his chilled fingers to the flame.

"Aren't you a little unreasonable, Julie?" he inquired, gently. "If Mrs. Parry didn't ask for you, I don't quite see what Dora could do but answer her questions."

"Me unreasonable? I like that! Mrs. Buel Parry came to this house to see me, but Dora was bound I shouldn't see her. Dora thinks"—she hesitated a moment, choking with her resentment—"she thinks I ain't Mrs. Parry's kind, and she was going to be considerate and keep us apart. Oh, yes! She thinks she knows what the upper crust wants. If I'm not Mrs. Parry's sort, I'd like to know why. You thought I was your sort fast enough, John Applegate!" and Julie threw back her dark head with a gesture that was very fine in its insolence. "I guess if Mrs. Parry and Mrs. Otis and that set are company for you, they're company for me. Of course you take Dora's side. You always do. I can tell you one thing. When I was Frazer MacDonald's wife I had some things I don't have now, for all you think you're so fine. MacDonald never would have stood by and seen me put upon. If folks wasn't civil to his wife, he knew the reason why. I might have done better than marry you — I might ——"

Julie stopped to take breath.

"Do you think I can make Mrs. Parry call on you if she doesn't want to, Julie?"

She shrugged her shoulders.

"What is the good of marrying a man who can't do anything for you?" she demanded. "It isn't any more than my due she should call, and you know it. She was thick enough with your first wife. And me to be treated so after all I've done for you and your children. I give you notice I'm going to Pullman to-morrow, and I'm going to stay till I get good and ready to come back. Maybe you'll find out who

makes this house comfortable for you, John
Applegate. Maybe you will."

And with this Julie slipped across the
room — she could not be ungraceful even
when she was most violent — and left it, shutting the door with emphasis.

There was deep silence between Applegate
and his daughter for a little while. Why
should either speak when there was really
nothing to say?

"Supper is on the table, father," observed
Dora, at last. "There is no use in letting
it get any colder," and still in silence they
went to their meal.

Julie MacDonald, born Dessaix, was the
daughter of a French market-gardener and of
a Spanish woman, the danseuse of a travelling troupe, who, when the company was left
stranded in an Indiana town, married this
thrifty admirer. The latter part of Julie's
childhood was passed in a convent school,
whence she emerged at fifteen a rabid little
Protestant with manners which the Sisters
had subdued slightly but had not been able
to make gentle. She learned the milliner's
trade, which she practised until, at twenty-two, she married Frazer MacDonald, a
gigantic, red-haired Scotch surveyor.

A few years after their marriage Mac-Donald went West, intending to establish himself and then send for Julie, whom he left meanwhile with her sister, the wife of a well-to-do mechanic living in Pullman. His train was wrecked somewhere in Arizona and the ruins took fire. MacDonald was reported among those victims whose bodies were too badly burned for complete identification, and though Julie refused to believe it at first, when the long days brought no tidings she knew in her heart that it was true.

She established herself at her old trade in one of the county towns of the Indiana prairie country, where she worked and prospered for three years before John Applegate asked her to marry him.

At the convent they had tried to teach her to worship God, but abstractions were not in Julie's line. Respectability was more tangible than righteousness, and deference to the opinion of the world an idea she could grasp. The worship of appearances came to be Julie's religion. Nothing could be more respectable than John Applegate, who was a hardware dealer and one of Belleplaine's leading merchants, and she accepted him with an almost religious enthusiasm.

AN INSTANCE OF CHIVALRY

The hardware business in a rich farming country is a good one. And then, in her own very unreasonable way, Julie was fond of Applegate.

"A little mouse of a man, yes," she said to herself, "but such a good little mouse! I'll have my way with things. When Mac-Donald was alive he had his way. Now — we'll see."

As for Applegate, he was just an average, unheroic, common-place man, such stuff as the mass of people are made of. Having decided to remarry for the sake of his children, he committed the not-uncommon inconsistency of choosing a woman who could never be acceptable to them and who suited himself entirely only in certain rare and unreckoning moods which were as remote from the whole trend of his existence as scarlet is from slate-color. But he found this untamed daughter of the people distinctly fascinating, and, with the easy optimism of one whose eyes are blinded by beauty, assured himself that it would come out all right.

His little daughter kissed him dutifully and promised to try to be a good girl when he told her he was going to bring a new mamma home, a pretty, jolly mamma, who would be almost a play-mate for her and Teddy, but secretly she felt a prescience that this was not the kind of mamma she wanted.

A few weeks after his marriage her father found her one day shaking in a passion of childhood's bitter, ineffectual tears. With great difficulty he succeeded in getting an explanation. It came in whispers, tremblingly.

"Papa, she—she says *bad words!* And this morning Teddy said one too. Oh, Papa"—the sobs broke out afresh — "how can he grow up to be *nice* and how am I going to get to be a lady—a lady like my own mamma—if nobody shows us how?"

Applegate dropped his head on his chest with a smothered groan. For himself he had not minded the occasional touches of profanity—to do her justice, they were rare — with which Julie emphasized her speech, for they had only seemed a part of the alien, piquantly un-English element in her which attracted him, but when Dora looked up at him with his dead wife's eyes he could not but acknowledge the justice of her tragic horror of "bad words."

"What have I done?" he asked himself as the child nestled closer, and then, "What shall I do?" for he found himself face to face with a future before whose problems he shrank helplessly.

One does not decide upon the merits of falcons according to the traditions of doves, and it would be quite as unjust to judge Julie Applegate from what came to be the standpoint of her husband and his children. There is no doubt that she made life hideous to them, but this result was accidental rather than intentional. There are those to whom the unbridled speech of natures without discipline is as much a matter of course as the sunshine and the rain. If to Applegate and Dora it was thunder-burst and cyclone, whose was the blame?

And if one is considering the matter of grievances, Julie certainly had hers. Most acute of all, she had expected to acquire a certain social prominence by her marriage, but was accorded only a grudging toleration by the circle to which the first Mrs. Applegate had belonged. This was the more grinding from the fact that in Belleplaine, as in all small towns of the great Middle-West, social distinctions are based upon personal quality and not upon position.

Then, there was Dora. From Julie's

point of view tempers were made to lose, but Dora habitually retained hers with a dignity which, while it endeared her to her father, only exasperated his wife. Julie developed an inordinate jealousy of the girl, and the love of the father and daughter became a rod to scourge them. With the most pacific intentions in the world it was impossible to divine what would or what would not offend Julie.

On the occasion of the family quarrel recorded, Julie departed for Pullman, according to her threat, and for a few days thereafter life was delightfully peaceful. Dora exhibited all sorts of housewifely aptitudes and solicitudes, the wheels of the household machinery moved smoothly, and the domestic amenities blossomed unchecked.

Julie had been gone a week, a week of golden Indian summer weather, when one day, as Applegate was leaving the house after dinner, he was met by the telegraph boy just coming in. He stopped at the gate and tore the message open. It was from Julie's brother-in-law, Hopson, and condensed in its irreverent ten words a stupefying amount of information. Applegate stared at it, unable to understand.

"MacDonald has come alive. Claims Julie. High old times. Come."

He crushed the yellow paper in his hands, and turning back, sat down heavily upon the steps of the veranda, staring stupidly ahead of him. If this were true, what did it mean to him? Out of the hundred thoughts assailing him one only was clear and distinct. It meant that he was free!

He turned the telegram over in his fingers, touching it with the look of one who sees visions.

Free. His home—his pretty home—his own again, with Dora, who grew daily more like her mother, as his little housekeeper. Free from that tempestuous presence which repelled even while it attracted. Free from the endless scenes, the tiresome bickerings, the futile jealousies, the fierce reproaches and the fierce caresses, both of which wearied him equally now. He had scarcely known how all these things which he bore in silence had worn and weighed upon him, but he knew at last. The measure of the relief was the measure of the pressure also. The tears trickled weakly down his cheeks, and he buried his face in his hands as if to hide his thankfulness even from himself. The prospect overwhelmed him. No boy's delight nor man's joy had ever been so sweet as this. When he looked up, the pale November sunlight seemed to hold for him a promise more alluring than that of all the Maytime suns that ever shone—the promise of a quiet life.

As he accustomed himself to this thought, there came others less pleasant. The preeminently distasteful features of the situation began to raise their heads and hiss at him like a coil of snakes. He shrank nervously from the gossip and the publicity. This was a hideous, repulsive thing to come into the lives of upright people who had thought to order their ways according to the laws of God and man. It was only Julie's due to say she had intended that. But it had come and must be met. Julie was MacDonald's wife, not his—not his. The only thing to be done was to accept the situation quietly. He knew that his own compensation was ample—no price could be too great to pay for this new joy of freedom—but he shivered a little when he thought of Julie with her incongruous devotion to the customary and the respectable. It would hurt Julie cruelly, but there was no one to blame and no help for it. And MacDonald could take her away into the far new West and make her forget this miserable interlude. He knew that for MacDonald, who was of a different fibre from himself, Julie's charm had been sufficient and enduring. Whatever might be the explanation of his long absence, Applegate did not doubt that the charm still endured. And, in the end, even they themselves would forget this unhappy time which was just ahead of them, and its memory would cease to seem a shame and become a regret, whose bitterness the passing years would lessen tenderly.

Having thus adjusted the ultimate outcome of the situation to suit the optimism of his mood, Applegate drew out his watch and looked at it. He had just time to make the necessary arrangements and catch the afternoon train for Chicago.

He telegraphed to Hopson, and as he left the train that evening he found the man awaiting him. The two shook hands awkwardly and walked away together in silence. It was only after they had gone a block or two that Hopson said:

"Well, I'm glad you've got here. We've

been having a picnic up at the house. Julie's been having the hysterics and MacDonald—you never knew MacDonald, did you?"

Applegate listened politely. He had a curious feeling that Julie and her hysterics were already very far away and unimportant to him, but he did not wish to be so brutal as to show this.

"When did MacDonald return and where has he been?" he asked, gravely.

"He got here yesterday. He says he had a shock or something in that accident—anyhow, he just couldn't remember anything, and when he come to he didn't know who he was, nor anything about himself, and all his papers and clothes had been burnt, so there was nothing to show anybody who he was. He could work, and he was all right most ways. Says he was that way till about six months ago, when a Frisco doctor got hold of him and did something to his head that put him right. He has papers from the doctor to show it's true. His case attracted lots of attention out there. Of course he wrote to Julie when he came to himself, but his letters went to our old address and she never got them. So then he started East to see about it. He says he's got into a good business and is going to do well."

There was a long silence. Presently Hopson began again, awkwardly:

"I don't know how you feel about it, but I think Julie'd ought to go back to him."

Applegate's heart began to beat in curious, irregular throbs; he could feel the pulsing of the arteries in his neck and there was a singing in his ears.

"Of course Julie agrees with you?" he said, thickly.

"Well, no; she don't. That's what she wanted me to talk to you about. She can't see it but one way. She says he died, or if he didn't it was the same thing to her, and she married you. She says nobody can have two husbands, and it's you who are hers. I told her the law didn't look at it that way, and she says then she must get a divorce from MacDonald and remarry you. MacDonald says if she brings suit on the ground of desertion he will fight it. He says he can prove it ain't been no wilful desertion. But probably he could be brought round if he saw she wouldn't go back to him anyhow. MacDonald wouldn't be spiteful. But he was pretty fond of Julie."

Applegate had stopped suddenly in the middle of Hopson's speech. Now he went forward rapidly, but he made no answer. Hopson scrutinized his face a moment before he continued:

"Julie says you won't be spiteful either. She says maybe she was a little hasty in what she said just before she came up here. But you know Julie's way."

"Yes," said Applegate, "I know Julie's way."

Hopson drew a breath of relief. He had at least discharged himself of his intercessory mission.

"I tell Julie she'd better put up with it and go with MacDonald. The life would be more the sort of thing she likes. But her head's set and she won't hear to anything Henriette or I say. You see, that's what Julie holds by, what she thinks is respectable. And it's about all she does hold by." He hesitated, groping blindly about in his consciousness for words to express his feeling that this passionate, reckless nature was only anchored to the better things of life by her fervent belief in the righteousness of the established social order.

AN INSTANCE OF CHIVALRY 63

"Julie thinks everything of being respectable," he concluded, lamely.

"Is it much farther to your house?" asked Applegate, dully.

"Right here," answered Hopson, pulling his key from his pocket.

They entered a crude little parlor whose carpet was too gaudy, and whose plush furniture was too obviously purchased at a bargain, but its air was none the less heavy with tragedy. A single gas-jet flickered in the centre of the room. On one side a great, broad-shouldered fellow sat doggedly with his elbows on his knees and his face buried in his hands. There was resistance in every line of his figure. On the sofa opposite was Julie in her crimson dress. As she lifted her face eagerly, Applegate noticed traces of tears upon it. Mrs. Hopson, who had been moving about the room aimlessly, a pale and ineffective figure between these two vivid personalities, came to a standstill and looked at Applegate breathlessly. For a moment no one spoke. Then Julie, baffled by the eyes she could not read, sprang to her feet and stretched out her hands with a vehement gesture.

"John Applegate, you'll put me right!

You will. I know you will. I can't go back to him! How can I?" Her hungry eyes scrutinized his still, inexpressive face.

"John, you aren't going to turn me off?" Her voice had a despairing passion in it. "You won't refuse to marry me if I get the divorce? Good God! You can't be such a devil. John! oh, John!"

Applegate sat down and looked at her apathetically. He was not used to being called a devil. Somehow it seemed to him the term was misapplied.

"Don't take on so, Julie," he said, quietly. The room seemed to whirl around him, and he added, with a palpable effort:

"I'll think it over and try to do what is best for both of us."

At that MacDonald lifted his sullen face from his hands for the first time and glanced across at the other man with blood-shot eyes. Then he rose slowly, his great bulk seeming to fill the room, and walking over to Applegate's chair stood in front of it looking down at him. His scrutiny was long. Once Applegate looked up and met his eyes, but he was too tired to bear their fierce light and dropped his own lids wearily.

MacDonald turned from him contemptuously and faced his wife, who averted her head.

"Look at me, Julie!" he cried, appealingly. "I am better worth it than he is. Good Lord! I don't see what you see in him. He's so *tame!* Let him go about his business. He's nobody. He don't want you. Come along with me and we'll lead a life! You shall cut a dash out there. I can make money hand over fist. It's the place for you. Come on!"

For a moment Julie's eyes glittered. The words allured her, but her old gods prevailed. She threw out her arms as if to ward off his proposal.

"No, no," she said, shrilly. "I cannot make it seem right. You were dead to me, and I married him. One does not go back to the dead. If I am your wife, what am I to him? It puts me in the wrong these two years. I cannot have it so, I tell you. I cannot have it so!"

Applegate felt faint and sick. Rising, he groped for the door. "I must have air," he said to Hopson, confusedly. "I will come back in a minute."

Once outside, the cool November night

refreshed him. He dropped down upon the doorstep and threw back his head, drinking in long breaths as he looked up at the mocking stars.

When he found at last the courage to ask himself what he was going to do, the answer was not ready. The decision lay entirely in his hands. He might still be free if he said the word; and as he thought of this he trembled. He had always tried to be what his neighbors called a straight man, and he wanted to be straight in this also. But where, in such a hideous tangle, was the real morality to be found? Surely not in acceding to Julie's demands! What claim had she upon the home whose simple traditions of peace and happiness she had trampled rudely under foot? Was it not a poor, cheap convention of righteousness which demanded he should take such a woman back to embitter the rest of his days and warp his children's lives? He rebelled hotly at the thought. That it was Julie's view of the ethical requirement of her position made it all the more improbable that it was really right. Surely his duty was to his children first, and as for Julie, let her reap the reward of her own temperament. The Lord God Himself could not say that this was unjust, for it is so that He deals with the souls of men.

It seemed to him that he had decided, but as he rose and turned to the door a new thought stabbed him so sharply that he dropped his lifted hand with a groan.

Where had been that sense of duty to his children, just now so imperative, in the days when he had yielded to Julie's charm against his better judgment? Had duty ever prevailed against inclination with him? Was it prevailing now?

High over all the turmoil and desperation of his thoughts shone out a fresh perception that mocked him as the winter stars had mocked. For that hour at least, the crucial one of his decision, he felt assured that in the relation of man and woman to each other lies the supreme ethical test of each, and in that relation there is no room for selfishness. It might be, indeed, that he owed Julie nothing, but might it not also be that the consideration he owed all womankind could only be paid through this woman he had called his wife? This was an ideal with which he had never had to reckon.

He turned and sat him down again to fight

the fight with a chill suspicion in his heart of what the end would be.

Being a plain man he had only plain words in which to phrase his decision when at last he came to it.

"I chose her and I'll bear the consequences of my choice," he said, "but I'll bear them by myself. His aunt will be glad to take Teddy, and Dora is old enough to go away to school." Then he opened the door.

Hopson and his wife had left the little parlor. Julie on the sofa had fallen into the deep sleep of exhaustion. MacDonald still sat there, with his head in his hands, and to him Applegate turned. At the sound of his step the man lifted his massive head and shook it impatiently.

"Well?" he demanded.

"The fact is, Mr. MacDonald, Julie and I don't get along very well together, but I don't know as that is any reason why I should force her to do anything that don't seem right to her. She thinks it would be more"— he hesitated for a word—"more nearly right to get a divorce from you and remarry me. As I see it now, it's for her to say what she wants, and for you and me to do it."

AN INSTANCE OF CHIVALRY

MacDonald looked at him piercingly.

"You know you'd be glad of the chance to get rid of her!" he exclaimed, excitedly. "In Heaven's name, then, why don't you make her come to me? You know I suit her best. You know she's my sort, not yours. She's as uncomfortable with you as you with her, and she'd soon get over the feeling she has against me. Man! There's no use in it! Why can't you give my own to me?"

"I can't say I don't agree with you," said Applegate, and the words seem to ooze painfully from his white lips, "but she thinks she'd rather not, and—it's for her to say."

A CONSUMING FIRE

A CONSUMING FIRE

He is a man who has failed in this life, and says he has no chance of success in another; but out of the fragments of his failures he has pieced together for himself a fabric of existence more satisfying than most of us make of our successes. It is a kind of triumph to look as he does, to have his manner, and to preserve his attitude toward advancing years—those dreaded years which he faces with pale but smiling lips.

If you would see my friend Hayden, commonly called by his friends the connoisseur, figure to yourself a tall gentleman of sixty-five, very erect still and graceful, gray-headed and gray-bearded, with fine gray eyes that have the storm-tossed look of clouds on a windy March day, and a bearing that somehow impresses you with an idea of the gracious and pathetic dignity of his lonely age.

I myself am a quiet young man, with but

one gift—I am a finished and artistic listener. It is this talent of mine which wins for me a degree of Hayden's esteem and a place at his table when he has a new story to tell. His connoisseurship extends to everything of human interest, and his stories are often of the best.

The last time that I had the honor of dining with him, there was present, besides the host and myself, only his close friend, that vigorous and successful man, Dr. Richard Langworthy, the eminent alienist and specialist in nervous diseases. The connoisseur evidently had something to relate, but he refused to give it to us until the pretty dinner was over. Hayden's dinners are always pretty, and he has ideals in the matter of china, glass, and napery which it would require a woman to appreciate. It is one of his accomplishments that he manages to live like a gentleman and entertain his friends on an income which most people find quite inadequate for the purpose.

After dinner we took coffee and cigars in the library.

On the table, full in the mellow light of the great lamp (Hayden has a distaste for gas), was a bit of white plush on which two large opals were lying. One was an intensely brilliant globe of broken gleaming lights, in which the red flame burned strongest and most steadily; the other was as large, but paler. You would have said that the prisoned heart of fire within it had ceased to throb against the outer rim of ice. Langworthy, who is wise in gems, bent over them with an exclamation of delight.

"Fine stones," he said; "where did you pick them up, Hayden?"

Hayden, standing with one hand on Langworthy's shoulder, smiled down on the opals with a singular expression. It was as if he looked into beloved eyes for an answering smile.

"They came into my possession in a singular way, very singular. It interested me immensely, and I want to tell you about it, and ask your advice on something connected with it. I am afraid you people will hardly care for the story as much as I do. It's—it's a little too rococo and sublimated to please you, Langworthy. But here it is:

"When I was in the West last summer, I spent some time in a city on the Pacific slope which has more pawnbrokers' shops and that sort of thing in full sight on the prominent streets than any other town of the same size and respectability that I have ever seen. One day, when I had been looking in the bazaars for something a little out of the regular line in Chinese curios and didn't find it, it occurred to me that in such a cosmopolitan town there might possibly be some interesting things in the pawn-shops, so I went into one to look. It was a common, dingy place, kept by a common, dingy man with shrewd eyes and a coarse mouth. Talking to him across the counter was a man of another type. Distinction in good clothes, you know, one is never sure of. It may be only that a man's tailor is distinguished. But distinction in indifferent garments is distinction indeed, and there before me I saw it. A young, slight, carelessly dressed man, his bearing was attractive and noteworthy beyond anything I can express. His appearance was perhaps a little too unusual, for the contrast between his soft, straw-colored hair and wine-brown eyes was such a striking one that it attracted attention from the real beauty of his face. The delicacy of a cameo is rough," added the connoisseur, parenthetically, "compared to the delicacy of outline and feature in a face that thought, and perhaps suffering, have worn away, but this is one of the distinctive attractions of the old. You do not look for it in young faces such as this.

"On the desk between the two men lay a fine opal—this one," said Hayden, touching the more brilliant of the two stones. "The younger man was talking eagerly, fingering the gem lightly as he spoke. I inferred that he was offering to sell or pawn it.

"The proprietor, seeing that I waited, apparently cut the young man short. He started, and caught up the stone. 'I'll give you—' I heard the other say, but the young man shook his head, and departed abruptly. I found nothing that I wanted in the place, and soon passed out.

"In front of a shop-window a little farther down the street stood the other man, looking in listlessly with eyes that evidently saw nothing. As I came by he turned and looked into my face. His eyes fixed me as the Ancient Mariner's did the Wedding Guest. It was an appealing yet commanding look, and I—I felt constrained to stop. I couldn't help it, you know. Even at my age one is not beyond feeling the force of an imperious attraction, and when you are past sixty you ought to be thankful on your knees for any emotion that is imperative in its nature. So I stopped beside him. I said: 'It is a fine stone you were showing that man. I have a great fondness for opals. May I ask if you were offering it for sale?'

"He continued to look at me, inspecting me calmly, with a fastidious expression. Upon my word, I felt singularly honored when, at the end of a minute or two, he said: 'I should like to show it to you. If you will come to my room with me, you may see that, and another;' and he turned and led the way, I following quite humbly and gladly, though surprised at myself.

"The room, somewhat to my astonishment, proved to be a large apartment—a front room high up in one of the best hotels. There were a good many things lying about which obviously were not hotel furnishings, and the walls, the bed, and even the floor were covered with a litter of water-color sketches. Those that I could see were admirable, being chiefly impressions of delicate and fleeting atmospheric effects.

"I took the chair he offered. He stood, still looking at me, apparently not in haste to show me the opals. I looked about the room.

"'You are an artist?' I said.

"'Oh, I used to be, when I was alive,' he answered, drearily. 'I am nothing now.' And then turning away he fetched a little leather case, and placed the two opals on the table before me.

"'This is the one I have always worn,' he said, indicating the more brilliant. 'That chillier one I gave once to the woman whom I loved. It was more vivid then. They are strange stones—strange stones.'

"He said nothing more, and I sat in perfect silence, only dreading that he should not speak again. I am not making you understand how he impressed me. In the delicate, hopeless patience of his face, in the refined, uninsistent accents of his voice, there was somehow struck a note of self-abnegation, of aloofness from the world, pathetic in any one so young.

"I am old. There is little in life that I care for. My interests are largely affected. Wine does not warm me now, and beauty seems no longer beautiful; but I thank Heaven I am not beyond the reach of a penetrating human personality. I have at least the ordinary instincts for convention in social matters, but I assure you it seemed not in the least strange to me that I should be sitting in the private apartment of a man whom I had met only half an hour before, and then in a pawnbroker's shop, listening eagerly for his account of matters wholly personal to himself. It struck me as the most natural and charming thing in the world. It was just such chance passing intercourse as I expect to hold with wandering spirits on the green hills of paradise.

"It was some time before he spoke again.

"'I saw her first,' he said, looking at the paler opal, as if it was of that he spoke, 'on the street in Florence. It was a day in April, and the air was liquid gold. She was looking at the Campanile, as if she were akin to it. It was the friendly grace of one lily looking at another. Later, I met her as one meets other people, and was presented to her. And after that the days went fast. I think she was the sweetest woman God ever made. I sometimes wonder how He came to think of her. Whatever you may have missed in life,' he said, lifting calm eyes to mine, and smiling a little, 'you whose aspect is so sweet, decorous, and depressing, whose griefs, if you have griefs, are the subtle sorrows of the old and unimpassioned'—I remember his phrases literally. I thought them striking and descriptive," confessed Hayden — "'I hope you have not missed that last touch of exaltation which I knew then. It is the most exquisite thing in life. The Fates must hate those from whose lips they keep that cup.' He mused awhile and added, 'There is only one real want in life, and that is comradeship — comradeship with the divine, and that we call religion; with the human, and that we call love.'

"'Your definitions are literature,' I ventured to suggest, 'but they are not fact. Believe me, neither love nor religion is exactly what you call it. And there are other things almost as good in life, as surely you must know. There is art, and there is work which is work only, and yet is good.'

"'You speak from your own experience?' he said, simply.

"It was a home thrust. I did not, and I knew I did not. I am sixty-five years old, and I have never known just that complete satisfaction which I believe arises from the perfect performance of distasteful work. I said so. He smiled.

"'I knew it when I set my eyes upon you, and I knew you would listen to me and my vaporing. Your sympathy with me is what you feel toward all forms of weakness, and in the last analysis it is self-sympathy. You are beautiful, not strong,' he added, with an air of finality, 'and I—I am like you. If I had been a strong man .... Christ!'

"I enjoyed this singular analysis of myself, but I wanted something else.

"'You were telling me of the opals,' I suggested.

"'The opals, yes. Opals always made me happy, you know. While I wore one, I felt a friend was near. My father found these in Hungary, and sent them to me—two perfect jewels. He said they were the twin halves of a single stone. I believe it to be true. Their mutual relation is an odd one. One has paled as the other brightened. You see them now. When they were both mine, they were of almost equal brilliancy. This,' touching the paler, 'is the one I gave to her. You see the difference in them now. Hers began to pale before she had worn it a month. I do not try to explain it, not even on the ground of the old superstition. It was not her fault that they made her send it back to me. But the fact remains; her opal is fading slowly; mine is burning to a deeper red.

Some day hers will be frozen quite, while mine—mine—' his voice wavered and fell on silence, as the flame of a candle fighting against the wind flickers and goes out.

"I waited many minutes for him to speak again, but the silence was unbroken. At last I rose. 'Surely you did not mean to part with either stone?' I said.

"He looked up as if from a dream. 'Part with them? Why should I sell my soul? I would not part with them if I were starving. I had a minute's temptation, but that is past now.' Then, with a change of manner, 'You are going?' He rose with a gesture that I felt then and still feel as a benediction. 'Good-by. I wish for your own sake that you had not been so like my poor self that I knew you for a friend.'

"We had exchanged cards, but I did not see or hear of him again. Last week these stones came to me, sent by some one here in New York of his own name—his executor. He is dead, and left me these.

"It is here that I want your counsel. These stones do not belong to me, you know. It is true that we are like, as like as blue and violet. But there is that woman somewhere— I don't know where; and I know no more of their story than he told me. I have not cared to be curious regarding it or him. But they loved once, and these belong to her. Do you suppose they would be a comfort or a curse to her? If—if—" the connoisseur evidently found difficulty in stating his position. "Of course I do not mean to say that I believe one of the stones waned while the other grew more brilliant. I simply say nothing of it; but I know that he believed it, and I, even I, feel a superstition about it. I do not want the light in that stone to go out; or if it should, or could, I do not want to see it. And, besides, if I were a woman, and that man had loved me so, I should wish those opals." Here Hayden looked up and caught Langworthy's amused, tolerant smile. He stopped, and there was almost a flush upon his cheek.

"You think I am maudlin—doting—I see," he said. "Langworthy, I do hope the Lord will kindly let you die in the harness. You haven't any taste for these innocent, green pastures where we old fellows must disport ourselves, if we disport at all. Now, I want to know if it would be—er—indelicate to attempt to find out who she is, and to restore the stones to her?"

Langworthy, who had preserved throughout his usual air of strict scientific attention, jumped up and began to pace the room.

"His name?" he said.

Hayden gave it.

"I know the man," said Langworthy, almost reluctantly. "Did any one who ever saw him forget him? He was on the verge of melancholia, but what a mind he had!"

"How did you know him, Langworthy!" asked Hayden, with pathetic eagerness.

"As a patient. It's a sad story. You won't like it. You had better keep your fancies without the addition of any of the facts."

"Go on," said Hayden, briefly.

"They live here, you know. He was the only son. He unconsciously acquired the morphine habit from taking quantities of the stuff for neuralgic symptoms during a severe protracted illness. After he got better, and found what had happened to him, he came to me. I had to tell him he would die if he didn't break it off, and would probably die if he did. 'Oh, no matter,' he said. 'What disgusts me is the idea that it has taken such hold of me.' He did break it off directly and absolutely. I never knew but one other man who did that thing. But between the pain and the shock from the sudden cessation of the drug, his mind was unbalanced for awhile. Of course the girl's parents broke off the engagement. I knew they were travelling with him last summer. It was a trying case, and the way he accepted his own weakness touched me. At his own request he carried no money with him. It was a temptation when he wanted the drug, you see. It must have been at some such moment, when he contemplated giving up the struggle, that you met him in the pawn-shop."

"I am glad I knew enough to respect him even there," murmured Hayden, in his beard.

"Oh, you may respect him, and love him if you like. He died a moral hero, if a mental and physical wreck. That is as good a way as any, or ought to be, to enter another life—if there is another life."

"And the woman?" asked the connoisseur.

"Keep the opals, Hayden; they and he are more to you than to her. She—in fact it is very soon—is to marry another man."

"Who is—"

"A gilded cad. That's all."

Langworthy took out his watch and looked at it. I turned to the table. What had happened to the dreaming stones? Did a light flash across from one to the other, or did my eyes deceive me? I looked down, not trusting what I saw. One opal lay as pale, as pure, as lifeless, as a moon-stone is. The other glowed with a yet fierier spark; instead of coming from within, the color seemed to play over its surface in unrestricted flame.

"See here!" I said.

Langworthy looked, then turned his head away sharply. The distaste of the scientific man for the inexplicable and irrational was very strong within him.

But the old man bent forward, the lamp-light shining on his white hair, and with a womanish gesture caught the gleaming opal to his lips.

"A human soul!" he said. "A human soul!"

AN UNEARNED REWARD

AN UNEARNED REWARD

It is the very last corner of the world in which you would expect to find a sermon. Overhead hang the Colorado skies, curtains of deepest, dullest cobalt, against which the unthreatening white clouds stand out with a certain solidity, a tangible look seen nowhere else save in that clear air. All around are the great upland swells of the mountains, rising endlessly, ridge beyond ridge, like the waves of the sea. In a hollow beside the glittering track is the one sign of human existence in sight—the sun-scorched, brown railway station. It is an insignificant structure planted on a high platform. There is a red tool-chest standing against the wall; a tin advertisement of somebody's yeast-cakes is nailed to the clap-boards; three buffalo hides, with horns still on them, hang over a beam by the coal-shed, and across the side of the platform, visible only to those approaching from the west, is written, in great, black letters :

THE WAGES OF SIN IS DEATH.

This legend had no place there on the September afternoon, some years ago, when Carroll Forbes stepped off the west-bound express as it halted a minute at the desolate spot. Because it looked to him like the loneliest place in all the world the notion seized him suddenly, as the train drew up beside the high platform, to catch up his valise and leave the car. He was looking for a lonely place, and looking helplessly. He snatched at the idea that here might be what he sought, as a drowning man at the proverbial straw.

When the train had gone on and left him there, already repenting tremulously of what might prove his disastrous folly, a man, who was possibly the station agent—if this were indeed a station—came limping toward him with an inquiring look.

Forbes was a handsome man himself, and thoroughly aware of the value of beauty as an endowment. He was conscious of a half-envious pang as he faced the blonde giant halting across the platform. This was, or had been, a singularly perfect specimen of the physical man. Over six feet in height, muscular, finely proportioned, fair-haired and fair-skinned, with a curling, blonde beard, and big, expressionless blue eyes, he looked as one might who had been made when the world was young, and there was more room for mighty men than now.

The slight, olive-skinned young man who faced him was conscious of the sudden feeling of physical disadvantage that comes upon one in the presence of imposing natural objects, for the man was as august in his way as the cliffs and canyons.

"I am a—an artist," said Carroll Forbes. "Is there any place hereabouts where I can get my meals and sometimes a bed, while I am sketching in the mountains?"

The man stared at him.

"Would it have been better if I had said I was a surveyor?" asked Forbes of his confused inner consciousness.

"We feed folks here sometimes—that is, my wife does. Mebbe you could have a shake-down in the loft. Or there's Connor's ranch off north a ways. But they don't care about taking in folks up there."

"Then, if you would ask your wife?" ventured Forbes, politely. "I shall not trouble you long," he added.

"Ellen!"

A woman appeared at the door, then moving slowly forward, stood at her husband's side, and the admiration Forbes had felt at the sight of the man flamed into sudden enthusiasm as he watched the wife. She was tall, with heavy, black hair, great eyes like unpolished jet, one of the thick white, smooth, perfectly colorless skins, which neither the sun nor the wind affect, and clear-cut, perfect features. Standing so, side by side, the two were singularly well worth looking at.

"What a regal pair!" was Forbes's internal comment; and while they conferred together he watched them idly, wondering what their history was, for of course they had one. It is safe to affirm that every human creature cast in the mould of the beautiful has, or is to have, one.

"She says you c'n stay," announced the man. "Just put those traps of yours inside, will you?" and, turning, he limped off the length of the platform at a call from somebody who had ridden up with jingling spurs.

Forbes, left to his own devices, picked up his valise, then set it down again and looked around him helplessly, wondering if there was a night train by which he could get away from this heaven-forsaken spot.

"If you want to see where you can sleep," said a voice at his side, "I will show you." It was the woman. She bent as she spoke to pick up some of his impedimenta, but he hastily forestalled her with a murmur of deprecation.

She turned and looked at him, and as he met her eyes it occurred to him that the indifference of her face was the indifference of the desert—arid and hopeless. The look she gave him was searching and impersonal; he saw no reason for it, nor for the slow, dark color that spread over her face, and there was less than no excuse for the way she set her lips and stretched a peremptory hand, saying, "Give me those," in tones that could not be disobeyed. To his own astonishment he surrendered them, and followed her meekly up a ladder-like flight of steps to the rough loft over the station. It was unfinished, but partitioned into two rooms. She opened the door of one of these apartments, silently set his luggage inside, and vanished down the stairs.

Forbes sat down on the edge of a broken chair and looked about him.

"Now, in heaven's name," he demanded of the barren walls, "what have I let myself in for, and why did I do it?"

To this question there seemed no sufficient answer, and for awhile he sat there fretting with the futile anxiety of a man who knows that his fate pursues him, who hopes that this turning or that may help him to evade it, yet always feels the benumbing certainty that the path he has taken is the shortest road to that he would avoid. When at last—recognizing that his meditations were unprofitable—he rose and went down the stairs, it was supper-time.

The woman was uncommunicative, but he could feel that her eyes were on him. The man—it occurred to Forbes that he had probably been drinking—was talkative. After the meal was over they went outside. Forbes, by way of supporting his pretence of being an artist, took out a pocket sketch-book and made notes of the values of the clouds and the outlines of the hills against the sky in a sort of artistic shorthand. The man Wilson sat down on a bench and began to talk. Between the exciting effects of the whiskey he had taken, the soothing influence of the cigar Forbes proffered him, and a natural talent for communicativeness, he presently went on to tell his own story. Forbes listened attentively. It seemed a part of the melodrama of the whole situation and was as unreal to him as the flaming miracle of the western skies or his own presence here.

"So the upshot of it all was that we just skipped out. She ran away with me."

It was a curious story. As Forbes listened he became aware that it was one with which he had occasionally met in the newspapers, but never in real life before. It was, apparently, the story of a girl belonging to a family of wealth and possibly of high social traditions—naturally he did not know what importance to attach to Wilson's boast that his wife belonged "to the top of the heap"—who had eloped with the man who drove her father's carriage.

The reasons for this revolt against the natural order of her life was obscure; there was, perhaps, too high a temper on her side and too strict a restraint on the part of her guardians. There was necessarily a total absence of knowledge of life; there was also the fact that the coachman was undoubtedly a fine creature to look at; there might have been a momentary yielding on the part of a naturally dramatic temperament to the impulse for the spectacular in her life.

But whatever the reasons, the result was the same. She had married this man and gone away with him, and they had drifted westward. And when they had gone so far west that coachmen of his stamp were no longer in demand, he took to railroading, and from brakeman became engineer; and finally, being maimed in an accident in which he had stood by his engine while the fireman jumped—breaking his neck thereby —he had picked up enough knowledge of telegraphy to qualify him for this post among the mountains. He and his handsome wife lived here and shared the everlasting solitude of the spot together, and occasionally fed stray travellers like this one who had dropped down on them to-day.

"He drinks over-freely and he swears profusely," mused Forbes, scrutinizing him, "but he is too big to be cruel, and he still worships her beauty as she, perhaps, once worshipped his; and he still feels an uncouth pride in all that she gave up for his sake."

It had never occurred to him before to wonder what the after-life of a girl who eloped with her father's servant might be like. He speculated upon it now. By just what process does a woman so utterly *déclassée* adjust herself to her altered position? Would she make it a point to forget, or would every reminder of lives, such as her own had been, be a turning of the knife in her wound? Would not a saving recollection of the little refinements of life cling longer to a weak nature than to a strong one under such circumstances?

This woman apparently gave tongue to no vain regrets, for her husband was exulting in the "grit" with which she had taken the fortunes of their life. "No whine about her," was his way of expressing his conviction that the courage of the thoroughbred was in her.

"No, sir; there's no whine about her. Un she's never been sorry, un, s'help me, she sha'n't never be," concluded Wilson. There were maudlin tears in his eyes.

"Few men can say that of their wives,"

said Forbes's smooth, sympathetic voice. "You are indeed fortunate."

While her husband was repeating the oft-told tale of their conjugal happiness, Ellen Wilson had done her after-supper work, and, slipping out of the door, climbed the short, rocky spur to the north of the station. Beyond the summit, completely out of sight and hearing, there was a little hollow that knew her well, but never had it seen her as it saw her now, when, throwing herself down, her face to the earth, she shed the most scalding tears of all her wretched years.

They were such little things this stranger had done—things so slight, so involuntary, so unconscious that they did not deserve the name of courtesies, but they were enough to open the flood-gates of an embittered heart. There was a world where all the men were deferential and all the women's lives were wrapped about with the fine, small courtesies of life—formal, but not meaningless. It had been her world once and now was so no longer.

Good or bad, she knew little and cared less, this man had come from that lost world of hers, as she was made aware by a thousand small signs, whose very existence she had forgotten; and silently, fiercely she claimed him as an equal.

"I—I too was—" Slow tears drowned the rest.

She could have told him how a *déclassée* grows used to it. She knew how the mind can adjust itself to any phase of experience, and had learned that what woman has undergone, woman can undergo—yes, and be strong about it. She knew how, under the impulse of necessity, the once impossible grows to be the accepted life, and the food that could not be swallowed becomes the daily bread.

When the struggle for existence becomes a hand-to-hand fight, traditions of one's ancestry do not matter, except, possibly, that some traditions bind you to strength and silence, while others leave you free to scream. She knew what it was to forget the past and ignore the future, and survey the present with the single-hearted purpose of securing three meals a day, if possible; two, if it were not.

She had forgotten with what facility she might the faces and scenes that once were dear to her. She had nothing to do with them any longer, as she knew. She might, perhaps, have heard their names without emotion. But, even in this day and generation and among this democratic people, in the soul of a woman bred as she had been the feeling for her caste is the last feeling that dies. And to her anguish she found that in her it was not yet dead.

The color died from the sky, and the stars came swiftly out.

She rose at last. It was time that she should be going. She stretched out the tired arms upon which she had been lying, looked at the patient hands which had long lost the beauty her face still kept, and lifted her eyes to the solemn sky.

"I shall die some day," she said, passionately. "No one can take that away from me. Thank Heaven, it is not one of the privileges a woman forfeits by marrying out of her station."

Forbes stayed three days longer; restless, wretched days whenever he thought of himself and his position; sunlit and serene whenever his facile temperament permitted him to forget them. He felt that he should be moving on, yet, having stopped, was at a loss how to proceed. Staying or going seemed equally difficult and dangerous.

He had no precedents to guide his action. Nothing in his previous life and training had ever fitted him to be a fugitive. He was, as he often reminded himself, not a fugitive from justice, but from injustice; which is quite another matter, but after all hardly more comfortable. He began to suspect that he might have been a fool to come away, but was too dazed to decide intelligently whether he should go forward or back. He was still in this undecided frame of mind on the morning of the third day.

Wilson and his wife performed by turns the duties of telegraph operator, with the difference that whereas she received by sound, he took the messages on paper. On the evening of the second day of Forbes's stay, Wilson, sitting alone in the office, received a message from Pueblo that startled him.

"Great Scott!" he said, and looked around to see if his wife was in sight. She was not, and on reflection he felt thankful. It would be better not to have her know. There were some things women, even plucky ones, made a fuss about. They were not fond of seeing criminals taken, for instance. So he answered the message, and having made the requisite copy locked that in the office safe. The long strip of paper, with its lines of dots and dashes, he crumpled carelessly and dropped into the wastebasket.

The next afternoon Mrs. Wilson, in the process of sweeping out the room, upset the waste-basket, and the crumpled piece of paper fell out and rolled appealingly to her feet. There were a dozen messages on the strip, but the last one riveted her eyes. She read it, then read it again; returned it to the waste-basket and sat down to think with folded hands in lap, her white face as inscrutable as the Sphinx. What should she do? Should she do anything?

The man might be a criminal or he might not. The fact that he was followed by detectives with papers for his arrest, who might be expected to arrive on the afternoon train, proved nothing to her mind. At the same time, criminal or none, if she interfered it might prove a dangerous experiment for her, and was sure to be a troublesome one. Why, then, should she interfere?

There was only one reason, but it was a reason rooted in the dumb depths of her being — the depths that this man's bearing had so disturbed. He was of her people; on her side—though it was the side that had cast her off. The faint, sweet memories of her earliest years pleaded for him; the enduring bitterness of that later life which she had lived sometimes forgetfully, sometimes—but this was rare — prayerfully, sometimes with long-drawn sighs, seldom with tears, always in silence, fought for him; the inextinguishable class-spirit fought for him—and fought successfully.

She looked at the clock. It lacked an hour of train-time. What she did must be done quickly.

She went out to her husband, loafing on the platform.

"I've got to go to Connor's, Jim. There's no butter and no eggs."

Wilson looked up carelessly. "All right," he said.

She went into the back room which served as kitchen and store-room and provided herself with a basket, into which she put meat and bread. As she left the station, Wilson came around to the side and called to her:

"You'll be back by supper-time, Ellen?"

The woman nodded, not looking back, and plunged on up the rocky spur.

When she found him, an hour later, Forbes was lying on a sunny slope indulging in the luxury of a day-dream. He was stretched out at full length, his arms under his head, the sketch-book that he had not used lying by his side unopened. For the life of him he could not feel that his position was serious, and the mountain-air and the sunshine intoxicated him.

"Once I get clear of this thing," he was saying to himself, "I'll come back here and buy me a ranch. Why should anybody who can live here want to live anywhere else?"

To him in this pastoral mood appeared the woman. There was that in her face which made him spring to his feet in vague alarm before she opened her lips.

"They're after you," she said. "You must be moving. Do you know what you want to do? What was your idea in stopping here? Have you any plans?"

He shook his head helplessly. "I thought perhaps—Mexico?"

"Mexico! But what you want just now is a place to hide in till they have given you up and gone along. After that you can think about Mexico. Come! I've heard the whistle. The train is in. You're all right if they don't start to look for you before supper-time, and I hardly think they will, for they'll expect you to come in. But if anybody should stroll out to look over the country, this place is in sight from the knoll beside the station. Come!"

Stumbling, he ran along beside her.

"I swear to you," he said between his labored breaths, "I did not do it. I am not unworthy of your help. But the evidence was damning and my friends told me to clear out. I may have been a fool to come — but it is done."

Her calm face did not change.

"You must not waste your breath," she warned. "We have two miles to go, and then I must walk to Connor's and get back by six o'clock, or there'll be trouble."

They were working their way back toward the station, but going farther to the east. She explained briefly that their objective point was the nearest canyon. She knew a place there where any one would be invisible both from above and below. It was fairly accessible — "if you are sure-footed," she warned. Here he might hide himself in safety for a day or two. She had brought him food. It would not be comfortable, but it was hardly a question of his comfort.

"You are very good," said Forbes, simply. "I don't want to give myself up now. You are very good," he repeated, wondering a little why she should take the pains.

She made no answer, only hastened on.

To Forbes the way seemed long. His feet grew heavy and his head bewildered. Was this really he, this man who was in flight from justice and dependent on the chance kindness of a stranger for shelter from the clutches of the law?

They reached the canyon and began to make their way slowly down and along its side. The woman led fearlessly over the twistings of a trail imperceptible to him. He followed dizzily. Suddenly she turned.

"It is just around this rock that juts out in front. Is your head steady? It falls off sheer below and the path is narrow."

"Go on," he said, and set his teeth.

The path was steep as well as narrow, and the descent below was sheer and far. Midway around the rocks a mist came over his eyes. He put up his hand, stumbled, fell forward and out, was dimly aware that he had fallen against his guide.

A crash and cry awoke the echoes of the canyon. Then silence settled over it again—dead silence—and the night came down.

Their bodies were not found until three days later. When the Eastern detectives had identified their man they proposed his burial, but Wilson turned from the place with the muscles of his throat working with impotent emotion, and a grim look about his mouth that lifted his lips like those of a snarling beast.

"Carrion! Let it lie," he said, with so dark a face that the men followed him silently, saying nothing more, and the two were left lying upon the ground which had drunk with impartial thirst the current that oozed from their jagged wounds.

The suspicions of primitive men are of a primitive nature. Those three days in which nothing had been seen or heard of his wife or Forbes had been a long agony to Wilson. And now that the end had come it seemed to him that his basest suspicions were confirmed. To his restricted apprehension there was but one passion in the world that could have sent his wife to this stranger's side, to guard and save him at her cost. So thinking, it seemed to him that swift justice had been done.

And that he might not forget, nor let his fierce thoughts of her grow more tender, the next day when the train had gone eastward and he was left alone to his desolation he took his brush and laboriously wrote across the end of the high platform, in great letters for all men to see and wonder at, the phrase he thought her fitting epitaph :

THE WAGES OF SIN IS DEATH.

And there it still stands, remaining in its stupid, brutal accusation the sole monument on earth of a woman's ended life.

HARDESTY'S COWARDICE

HARDESTY'S COWARDICE

I

STRAIGHT on before them stretched the street, a wide and unobstructed way at first, but narrowing a little farther on, where there were, besides, buildings going up, and great piles of lumber standing far out in the road, and heaps of sand, and mortar-beds. Could he possibly get the horses under control before they reached those cruel lumber piles, where to be thrown meant death or worse? They were running wildly, and it was down hill all the way. She did not believe that human strength could do it, not even Neil's, and he was as strong as he was tender. She looked down at his hands and noticed how white the knuckles were, and how the veins stood out, and then she bent her head that she might not see those fatal obstructions in their way, and clasped her hands as tightly as her lips. She found herself senselessly repeating, over and over, as if it were a charm, "*Broad is the way . . . that leadeth to destruction.*"

It was a June morning, cool and sweet. If ever, life is dear in June. Her eyes fell on the great bunch of white roses in her lap. He had put them in her hands just as they were starting, and then had bent suddenly and left a quick kiss on the hands. It was only the other day he had told her that he had never, from the very first hour they met, seen her hands without longing to fill them with flowers. Would she be pleased to take notice, now that he possessed the right, he meant to exercise it?

Poor roses! Must they be crushed and mangled, too? She did not like the thought of scarlet stains upon their whiteness, and with some wild thought of saving them—for were they not his roses?—she flung them with a sudden gesture into the street.

"Oh, Christ!" she cried, voicelessly, "spare both of us—or neither!"

It was just then that the horses swerved and reared, the carriage struck something in the road and tilted sharply to the right. She clutched the side involuntarily and kept her seat. When, a second later, the carriage had righted itself, and the horses, more terrified still and now wholly uncontrolled, were dashing forward again, the place beside her was vacant, and the reins were dragging on the ground.

She shut her eyes and waited. It was not long to wait. There came a crash, a whirl, and then unconsciousness.

The evening papers contained an account of the fortunate escape from serious disaster of Mr. Neil Hardesty and Miss Mildred Fabian, who were on their way to a field meeting of the Hambeth Historical Society when the young blooded horses Mr. Hardesty was driving took fright at a bonfire at at the corner of State and Market Streets, and started to run. Owing to the sharp down-grade at this point, their driver was unable to control them. After keeping their course in a mad gallop down State Street for a quarter of a mile, the carriage struck an obstruction, tipped, and Mr. Hardesty was thrown out, being severely bruised, but sustaining no serious injuries. The horses continued running wildly for two blocks more, when one of them ran against a lamp-post and was knocked down, upsetting the carriage and throwing Miss Fabian out. She was picked up unconscious, but beyond a cut on the head was also fortunately uninjured. Mr. Hardesty and Miss Fabian were to be congratulated upon the results of the runaway, as such an accident could hardly occur once in a hundred times without more serious, and probably fatal, consequences.

It was some two weeks later that the family physician, consulting with Mrs. Fabian in the hall, shook his head and said he did not understand it; there was no apparent reason why Miss Mildred should not have rallied immediately from the accident. The shock to her nervous system had doubtless been greater than he had at first supposed. Still, she had been in sound health, and there seemed no sufficient cause for her marked weakness and depression. He would prepare a tonic and send it up.

Meeting Neil Hardesty, himself an unfledged medical student, entering the house, the doctor stopped to observe:

"You must try to rouse your fiancée a little. Can't you cheer her up, Hardesty? She seems very much depressed nervously. Perhaps it is only natural after such a close shave as you had. I did not care to look death in the face at that age. It sometimes startles young people and happy ones."

Neil shook his head with an anxious look.

"It is not that," he said, "for she is half an angel already. But I will do my best," and he passed on through the broad, airy, darkened hall to the high veranda at the back of the house, where he knew he should find her at that hour.

The veranda overlooked the garden, blazing just then with the flowers of early July. She was lying languidly in her sea-chair; there were books around her, but she had not been reading; and work, but she had not been sewing. One hand was lifted shading her face. The lines around her mouth were fixed as if she were in pain.

He came forward quickly and knelt beside the chair. He was carrying some brilliant clusters of scarlet lilies, and he caught the small and rather chilly hand, and held it over them as if to warm it in their splendid flame.

"Do you know that you look cold?" he demanded. "I want you to look at these and hold them till you are warmed through and through. What an absurd child it is to look so chilly in July!"

She raised her eyes and let them rest on him with a sudden radiant expression of satisfaction.

"It is because you are so unkind as to go away—occasionally," she remarked. "Do I ever look cold or unhappy or dissatisfied while you are here?"

"Once or twice in the last two weeks you have been all of that. Sweetheart, I must know what it means. Don't you see you must tell me? How can one do anything for you when one doesn't know what is the matter? And I am under orders to see that you get well forthwith. The doctor has given you up—to me!"

He was startled when, instead of the laughing answer for which he looked, she caught her breath with half a sob.

"Must I tell you?" she said. "Neil, I do not dare! When you are here I know it is not so. It is only when you are away from me that the hideous thought comes. And I fight it so! It is only because I am tired with fighting it that I do not get strong."

"Dear, what can you mean?"

She shook her head.

"It is too horrible, and you would never forgive me, though I know it cannot be true. Oh, Neil, Neil, *Neil!*"

"Mildred, this is folly. I insist that you tell me at once." His tone had lost its tender playfulness and was peremptory now. "Don't you see that you are torturing me?" he said.

She looked at him helplessly.

"That day," she said, reluctantly, "when the carriage tipped and you went out, I thought—I thought you jumped. Neil, don't look so; I knew you could not have done it, and yet I can't get rid of the thought, and it tortures me that I can think it—of you. Oh, I have hurt you!"

He was no longer kneeling beside her, but had risen and was leaning against one of the pillars of the veranda, looking down at her with an expression she had never dreamed of seeing in his eyes when they rested on her face. He was white to the lips.

"You thought that? You have thought it these two weeks?"

"I tell you it is torture. Neil, say you did not, and let me be at rest."

"And you ask me to *deny* it? You?"

His voice was very bitter. "I wonder if you know what you are saying?"

"Neil, Neil, say you did not!"

He set his teeth.

"Never!"

He broke the silence which followed by asking, wearily, at last:

"What was your idea in telling me this, Mildred? Of course you knew it was the sort of thing that is irrevocable."

"I knew nothing except that I must get rid of the thought."

"Can't you imagine what it is to a man to be charged with cowardice?"

"I charge nothing. But if you would only deny it!"

"Oh, this is hopeless!" he said, with an impatient groan. "It is irremediable. If I denied it, you would still doubt; but even if you did not, I could never forget that you had once thought me a coward. There are some things one may not forgive."

Silence again.

"And my—my wife must never have doubted me."

She raised her eyes at last.

"If you are going, pray go at once," she said. "I am too weak for this."

She said it, but she did not mean it. After all, it was the one impossible thing on earth that anything should come between them. Surely she could not alter the course of two lives by five minutes of unguarded hysterical speech or a week or two of unfounded fretting.

But he took up his hat, and turned it in his hands.

"As you wish," he said, coldly, and then "Good-morning," and was gone.

II

"I THINK that is all," said the hurried, jaded doctor to the Northern nurse. "The child is convalescent—you understand about the nourishment?—and you know what to do for Mrs. Leroy? I shall bring some one who will stay with her husband within the hour."

Outside was the glare of sun upon white sand—a pitiless sun, whose rising and setting seemed the only things done in due order in all the hushed and fever-smitten city. Within was a shaded green gloom and the anguished moaning of a sick woman.

Mildred Fabian, alone with her patients and the one servant who had not deserted the house, faced her work and felt her heart rise with exultation — a singular, sustaining joy that never yet had failed her in the hour of need. The certainty of hard work, the consciousness of danger, the proximity of death — these acted always upon her like some subtle stimulant. If she had tried to explain this, which she did not, she would perhaps have said that at no other time did she have such an overwhelming conviction of the soul's supremacy as in the hours of human extremity. And this conviction, strongest in the teeth of all that would seem most vehemently to deny it, was to her nothing less than intoxicating.

She was not one of the women to whom there still seems much left in life when love is gone. To be sure, she had the consolations of religion and a certain sweet reasonableness of temperament which prompted her to pick up the pieces after a crash, and make the most of what might be left. But she was obliged to do this in her own way. She was sorry, but she could not do it in her mother's way.

When she told her family that her engagement was at an end, that she did not care to explain how the break came, and that if they meant to be kind they would please not bother her about it, she knew that her mother would have been pleased to have her take up her old life with a little more apparent enthusiasm for it than she had ever shown before. To be a little gayer, a little more occupied, a little prettier if possible, and certainly a little more fascinating—that was her mother's idea of saving the pieces. But Mildred's way was different, and after dutifully endeavoring to carry out her mother's conception of the conduct proper to the circumstances with a dismal lack of success, she took her own path, which led her through a training school for nurses first, and so, ultimately, to Jacksonville.

The long day wore slowly into night. The doctor had returned very shortly with a man, whether physician or nurse she did not know, whom he left with Mr. Leroy. The little maid, who had been dozing in the upper hall, received some orders concerning the preparation of food which she proceeded to execute. The convalescent child rested well. The sick woman passed from the first to the second stage of the disease and was more quiet. The doctor came again after nightfall. He looked at her charges wearily, and told Mildred that the master of the house would not rally.

"He is my friend, and I can do no more for him," he said, almost with apathy.

The night passed as even nights in sick-rooms will, and at last it began to grow toward day. The nurse became suddenly conscious of deadly weariness and need of rest. She called the servant and left her in charge, with a few directions and the injunction to call her at need, and then stole down the stairs to snatch, before she rested, the breath of morning air she craved.

As she stood at the veranda's edge in the twilight coolness and twilight hush watching the whitening sky, there came steps behind her, and turning, she came face to face with Neil Hardesty. She stared at him with unbelieving eyes.

"Yes, it is I," he said.

"You were with Mr. Leroy?" she asked. "Are you going?"

"My work is over here," he answered, quietly. "I am going to send—some one else."

She bent her head a second's space with

the swift passing courtesy paid death by those to whom it has become a more familiar friend than life itself, then lifted it, and for a minute they surveyed each other gravely.

"This is like meeting you on the other side of the grave," she said. "How came you here? I thought you were in California."

"I thought you were in Europe."

"I was for awhile, but there was nothing there I wanted. Then I came back and entered the training school. After this is over I have arranged to join the sisterhood of St. Margaret. I think I can do better work so."

"Let me advise you not to mistake your destiny. You were surely meant for the life of home and society, and can do a thousand-fold more good that way."

"You do not know," she answered, simply. "I am very happy in my life. It suits me utterly. I have never been so perfectly at peace."

"But it will wear you out," he murmured.

She looked at him out of her great eyes, surprisedly. It was a look he knew of old.

"Why, I expect it to," she answered.

There was a little silence before she went on, apparently without effort:

"I am glad to come across you again, for there is one thing I have wanted to say to you almost ever since we parted, and it has grieved me to think I might never be able to say it. It is this. While I do not regret anything else, and while I am sure now that it was best for both of us—or else it would not have happened—I have always been sorry that the break between us came in the way it did. I regret that. It hurts me still when I remember of what I accused you. I am sure I was unjust. No wonder you were bitter against me. I have often prayed that that bitterness might pass out of your soul, and that I might know it. So—I ask your forgiveness for my suspicion. It will make me happier to know you have quite forgiven me."

He did not answer. She waited patiently.

"Surely"—she spoke with pained surprise—"surely you can forgive me now?"

"*Oh, God!*"

She looked at his set face uncomprehending. Why should it be with such a mighty effort that he unclosed his lips at last? His voice came forced and hard.

"I—I did it, Mildred. I was the coward that you thought me. I don't know what insensate fear came over me and took possession of me utterly, but it was nothing to the fear I felt afterwards — for those two weeks—that you might suspect me of it. And when I knew you did I was mad with grief and anger at myself, and yet—it seems to me below contempt—I tried to save my miserable pride. But I have always meant that you should know at last."

She looked at him with blank uncomprehension.

"I did it," he repeated, doggedly, and waited for the change he thought to see upon her face. It came, but with a difference.

"You—you did it?" for the idea made its way but slowly to her mind. "Then" —with a rush of feeling that she hardly understood, and an impetuous, tender gesture —"then let me comfort you."

It was the voice of the woman who had loved him, and not of any Sister of Charity, however gracious, that he heard again, but he turned sharply away.

"God forbid," he said, and she shrank from the misery in his voice; "God forbid that even you should take away my punishment. Don't you see? It is all the comfort I dare have, to go where there is danger and to face death when I can, till the day comes when I am not afraid, for I am a coward yet."

She stretched her hands out toward him blindly. I am afraid that she forgot just then all the boasted sweetness of her present life, her years of training, and her coming postulancy at St. Margaret's, as well as the heinousness of his offence. She forgot everything, save that this was Neil, and that he suffered.

But all that she, being a woman and merciful, forgot, he, being a man and something more than just, remembered.

"Good-by, and God be with you," he said.

"Neil!" she cried. "Neil!"

But his face was set steadfastly toward the heart of the stricken city, and he neither answered nor looked back.

The future sister of St. Margaret's watched him with a heart that ached as she had thought it could never ache again. All the hard-won peace of her patient years, which she thought so secure a possession, had gone at once and was as though it had not been; for he, with all his weaknesses upon him, was still the man she loved.

"Lord, give him back to me!" she cried, yet felt the cry was futile.

Slowly she climbed the stairs again, wondering where was the courage and quiet confidence that had sustained her so short a time ago.

Was it true, then, that heaven was only excellent when earth could not be had? She was the coward now. In her mind there were but two thoughts—the desire to see him again, and a new, appalling fear of death.

She re-entered the sick-room where the girl was watching her patients with awed eyes.

"You need not stay here," she said, softly. "I cannot sleep now. I will call you when I can."

"THE HONOR OF A GENTLEMAN"

"THE HONOR OF A GENTLEMAN"

I

BECAUSE there was so little else left him to be proud of, he clung the more tenaciously to his pride in his gentle blood and the spotless fame of his forefathers. There was no longer wealth nor state nor position to give splendor to the name, but this was the less sad in that he himself was the sole survivor of that distinguished line. He was glad that he had no sisters — a girl should not be brought up in sordid, ignoble surroundings, such as he had sometimes had to know; as for brothers, if there had been two of them to make the fight against the world shoulder to shoulder, life might have seemed a cheerier thing; but thus far he had gotten on alone. And the world was not such an unkindly place, after all. Though he was a thousand miles away from the old home, in this busy Northwestern city where he and his were unknown, he was not without friends; he knew a few nice people. He had money enough to finish his legal studies; if there had not been enough, he supposed he could have earned it somehow; he was young and brave enough to believe that he could do anything his self-respect demanded of him. If it sometimes asked what might seem to a practical world fantastic sacrifices at his hands, was he not ready to give them? At least, had he not always been ready before he met Virginia Fenley?

She reminded him of his mother, did Virginia, though no two women in the world were ever fundamentally more different. Nevertheless, there was a likeness between the little pearl-set miniature which he cherished, showing Honora Le Garde in the prime of her beauty, and this girl who looked up at him with eyes of the self-same brown. Surely, Virginia should not be held responsible for the fact that a slender, graceful creature with yellow hair and dark-lashed hazel eyes, with faint pink flushes coming and going in her cheeks, and the air of looking out at the world with indifference from a safe and sheltered distance, was Roderick

Le Garde's ideal of womanhood, and that he regarded her, the representative of the type, as the embodiment of everything sweetest and highest in human nature. Virginia's physique, like Roderick's preconceptions of life and love and honor, was an inheritance, but a less significant one; it required an effort to live up to it, and Virginia was not fond of effort.

His feeling for her was worship. Virginia had not been looking on at the pageant (Roderick would have called it a pageant) of society very long, but she was a beautiful girl and a rich one; therefore she had seen what called itself love before.

As an example of what a suitor's attitude should be, she preferred Roderick's expression of devotion to that of any man she knew. He made her few compliments, and those in set and guarded phrase; except on abstract topics, his speech with her was restrained to the point of chilliness; even the admiration of his eyes was controlled as they met hers. But on rare occasions the veil dropped from them, and then—Virginia did not know what there was about these occasions that she should find them so fascinating; that she should watch for them and wait for them, and even try to provoke them, as she did.

Worship is not exactly the form of sentiment of which hopelessness can be predicated, but Roderick was human enough to wish that the niche in which his angel was enshrined might be in his own home. He let her see this one day in the simplicity of his devotion.

"Not that I ask for anything, you understand," he added, hastily. "I could not do that. It is only that I would give you the knowledge that I love you, as—as I might give you a rose to wear. It honors the flower, you see," he said, rather wistfully.

She lifted her eyes to his, and he wondered why there should flash across his mind a recollection of the flowers she had worn yesterday, a cluster of Maréchal Niels that she had raised to her lips once or twice, kissing the golden petals. She made absolutely no answer to his speech, unless the faintest, most evanescent of all her faint smiles could be called an answer. But she was not angry, and she gave him her hand at parting.

In spite of her silence she thought of his words. The little that she had to say upon the subject she said to her father as they were sitting before the library fire that evening.

John Fenley was a prosperous lumberman, possessed of an affluent good nature which accorded well with his other surroundings in life. Virginia was his only child, and motherless. She could not remember that her father ever refused her anything in his life; and certainly he had never done so while smoking his after-dinner cigar.

"Papa," she began, in her pretty, deliberate way—"papa, Roderick Le Garde is in love with me."

Her father looked up at her keenly. She was not blushing, and she was not confused. He watched a smoke-ring dissolve, then answered, comfortably,

"Well, there is nothing remarkable about that."

"That is true," assented Virginia. "The remarkable thing is that I like him—a little." Her eyes were fixed upon the fire. There was a pause before she went on. "I have never liked any of them at all before, as you know very well. I never expect to— very much. Papa, you afford me everything I want; can you afford me Roderick Le Garde?"

"Do you know what you are asking, Virginia, or why?" he said, gravely.

"I have thought it over, of course. Couldn't you put him in charge at one of the mills or somewhere on a comfortable number of thousands a year? Of course I can't starve, you know, and frocks cost something."

"My daughter is not likely to want for frocks," said John Fenley, frowning involuntarily. "You did not take my meaning. I wish your mother were here, child."

"I am sufficiently interested, if that is what you mean," said Virginia, still tranquilly. "He is different, papa; and I am tired of the *jeunesse dorée*. Perhaps it is because I am so much *dorée* myself that they bore me. Roderick has enthusiasms and ideals; I am one of them; I like it. You, papa, love me for what I am. It is much more exciting to be loved for what one is not."

Her father knit his brows and smoked in silence for a few minutes. Virginia played with the ribbons of her pug.

"Marylander, isn't he?"

"Something of the sort; I forget just what."

"H'm!"

"Le Garde isn't a business man," John Fenley said, at length.

"Isn't he?" asked Virginia, politely smothering a yawn.

"Is he? You know enough about it to know how important it is that any man who is to work into my affairs, and ultimately to take my place, should know business and mean business, Virgie. It is a long way from poverty to wealth, but a short one from wealth to poverty."

"Yes," said Virginia, "I know; but I also know enough about it to be sure that I could manage the business if it became necessary. You and I are both business men, dear. Let us import a new element into the family."

Fenley laughed proudly. "By Jove! I believe you could do it!" A little further silence; then, "So your heart is set on this, daughter?"

"Have I a heart?" asked Virginia, sedately, rising and leaning an elbow on the mantel as she held up one small, daintily slippered foot to the blaze.

II

Long afterward he used to wonder how it had ever come to pass—that first false step of his, the surrender of his profession, and so of his liberty. Before middle life a man sometimes forgets the imperious secret of the springs that moved his youthful actions. In reality, the mechanism of his decision was very simple.

"How can I give up my profession?" he asked Virginia.

She smiled up into his eyes, her own expressing a divine confidence. "But how can you give up me?"

Though his doubts were not thereby laid to rest, the matter was practically settled, and it was understood between them that he was to accept her father's unnecessarily liberal offer, and take his place in John Fenley's business as his own son might have done. This may have been unwise, but it was not unnatural, and if there was any unwisdom in the proceeding, it was apparent to no eyes but Roderick's own. Other people said what other people always say under such circumstances—that young Le Garde was in luck; that he would have a "soft snap" of it as John Fenley's son-in-law; that he had shown more sagacity in feathering his own nest than could have been expected of such an impractical young fellow. They did not understand his chill reserve when congratulated on this brilliant bit of success in life. If they had spoken of his good fortune in being loved by Virginia, that was something a man could understand. The gods might envy Virginia's lover, but that he, Roderick Le Garde, should be congratulated on becoming John Fenley's son-in-law was intolerable.

He by no means pretended to scorn money, however, and he felt as strongly as did Fenley that Virginia must have it. Luxury was her natural atmosphere—any woman's perhaps, but surely hers. Other men sacrificed other things for the women that they loved. He gave up his proud independence and his proper work, and was sublimely sure that Virginia understood what the sacrifice cost him.

But it was true that he was not a business man by nature, and his first few years in John Fenley's service were not the exacting drill which would have given him what he lacked. Although he conscientiously endeavored to carry his share of the burden and do well what fell to him to do, the fact was that John Fenley was a great deal too energetic and too fond of managing his own affairs to give up any duties to another which he could possibly perform for himself. Thus Roderick's various positions were always more or less of sinecures as far as responsibility was concerned, and he had a large margin of leisure as well as a sufficient amount of money to devote to good books and good horses, pursuits which met the approval of his father-in-law as being the "tastes of a gentleman."

John Fenley did not show his usual foresight, certainly, in encouraging Roderick to be in the business and not of it; but then he confidently expected to live to settle up all his own affairs, and turn his large fortune into a shape in which it would be more easily managed than in its primitive form of timber lands and saw-mills. No one could have anticipated his death, which occurred in the prime of his active life, some five years after his daughter's marriage.

Even then his son-in-law hardly took the position expected of him. His long habit of standing aside was not easily overcome, and Mrs. Le Garde, who had a taste for affairs, and Mr. Rogers, her father's private secretary, had actually more to do with certain important transactions than the nominal head of the business.

One of these transactions was as follows:

"Mrs. Le Garde," said Mr. Rogers, being shown into the library one chilly afternoon in early October, "Macomb has cabled from Vienna to his agent here to close with us for that tract of Michigan timber, paying the price agreed upon for cash. I have had the papers ready for some time, and they only want signing. If you can come down town at once——"

Virginia looked down at her tea-gown, and then at the cheerful little fire on the hearth, and her novel lying face downward on the easiest chair.

"Won't to-morrow morning do as well?" she asked, languidly.

"If you will permit me to say so, by no means, Mrs. Le Garde," said Mr. Rogers, suavely.

Something in his manner attracted her attention.

"Why not?" she demanded.

Mr. Rogers looked at the fire for a moment before replying. "You wish to realize upon the land, you see," he observed, vaguely. "The cablegram was received this morning. Macomb's agent has no choice but to act on it now. By to-morrow, or next day at the farthest, there may be reasons apparent which would justify him in declaring the deal off. It is worth your while, *and it should be made worth mine,*" said Mr. Rogers, leaning upon the words, "to see that the matter is settled this afternoon. I have private advices that forest fires have started in northern Michigan — ah — somewhat in this vicinity, and their spread is greatly to be feared. I have not mentioned this to Mr. Le Garde."

Mrs. Le Garde hesitated a moment. It would be charitable to suppose that she did not understand the situation so lightly sketched in, but I am afraid she did. Mr. Rogers did not raise his eyes.

"Oh, well," she said, carelessly, "to-day or to-morrow, it doesn't signify. If you will have a notary and Macomb's agent at Mr.

Le Garde's office in half an hour, Mr. Rogers, I will be there."

So it was that the papers were executed and payment made that afternoon. The next day but one, "Forest Fires. Danger to Lumber Interests in Michigan," was a prominent head-line in the morning papers.

When Macomb came home from Vienna to look after his own affairs a month later he found himself the owner of a diminished bank account and some hundreds of acres of smoking pine-stumps.

He made a trip to northern Michigan to survey these latter possessions, and while there succeeded in securing some interesting statements which it pleased him to call "facts." Armed with these, he went to Roderick Le Garde, and laid his case before him.

"First of all, I want to say that I have always thought you an honest man, Le Garde," he observed, "and I wish to say that I am bringing no personal accusations, though the case looks black for you. But I know your man Rogers is a d——d scoundrel, though I fail to see how the sale could profit him, apart from its advantages to you. But you will see I have proof that he was well-informed on the day the transfer took place that that tract of timber was already on fire in a dozen places, and nothing on earth could save it from destruction. I call that obtaining money under false pretences, and I warn you if you don't desire to repurchase the entire tract at the price I paid for it, that I propose to see at once what the courts will call it."

"Much obliged for your good opinion of me," said Le Garde, dryly. "I have perfect confidence in Rogers"—this was not strictly true, but Roderick was angry—"and none at all in your so-called 'proofs.' I shall do a little investigating for myself. If I find, as I believe, that Rogers had no other information in the matter than I myself possessed, and that you have met with your losses only in the ordinary course of events, you may bring as many suits as you like, and rest assured that the Fenley estate will fight them to the last dollar. If it is otherwise—but nothing else is possible! Good-morning, sir."

III

"Virginia! Do you mean that Rogers actually approached *you* in the matter?"

Mrs. Le Garde moved uneasily under the scorching light in her husband's eyes. It was a new experience to see anything but tenderness in his face, but she respected him for the look she resented.

"He had to consult some one, of course. You have given no attention to things of late." Her voice was irritatingly even. "Papa always said you had no head for business."

"Your father was an honest man, Virginia," cried her husband, desperately. "He would have been the last person in the world to attempt to increase his gains dishonestly."

"I see nothing dishonest about it," said Virginia, coldly. "I really think Roderick, under all the circumstances, it would have been more appropriate if you had learned something about money in the last seven years—besides how to spend it."

Nothing dishonest!

"Don't you understand," demanded

Le Garde, in a terrible voice, "that the 'commission' you paid Rogers was blackmail, the price of his 'news' and his silence?"

Mrs. Le Garde shrugged her shoulders.

Roderick rose dumbly. He knew all that he need. The room whirled round him. How he made his way out of the house he did not know. Had he served seven years —for this? The fair house of his life, built up on the insubstantial foundations of a woman's silence and her sweet looks, was tumbling about his ears. She whom he had made his wife, who wore the name he honored though it was his own, whom he had worshipped as woman never yet was worshipped, had failed in common honesty, and taunted him with the life he had led for her sake. She had betrayed him into a shameful position. That restitution was an easy matter and might be a secret one did not make the case less hard. He could have defended her had she been disgraced in the world's eyes, but how might he defend her from himself?

It was a raw November night. As he went swiftly on, he felt the river-mists sweep soft against his face. He wrung his helpless hands. "Oh, God! It is dishonor! What shall I do? What shall I do?"

No help in the murky sky above him; none in the home whose lights lay behind; none in the river that rushed along beneath the bluff—that was the refuge of a coward and a shirk. Had he not already shirked too much in life?

What must he do? He tried to think collectedly, but in his pain he could not. There were visions before his eyes. He saw Virginia as she had seemed to him seven years ago—five years—yesterday—to-night. Was it true that he had never really seen her till to-night?

Oh, that brave, lost youth of his! His strong, light-hearted youth, with its poverty, its pride, and its blessed, blessed freedom! If he could but go back to it, and feel himself his own man once more, with his life before him to be lived as he had planned it. How was it that he had become entangled with a soul so alien to his own? And what did a man do when he reached a point from which he could not go back, yet loathed to go forward?

He tramped on and on through the drizzling November darkness. Gradually the tumult in his heart was stilled. He became aware that the air was cold, that he was splashed with mud and rain, that he had no hat, and wore only thin evening clothes. He turned at last, his teeth chattering in his head, and plodded back.

Two things grew clear before his mind—he must settle with Macomb to-morrow, and he must henceforth assume the control of John Fenley's affairs which he had hitherto nominally possessed. Thank Heaven for the gift of work!

And Virginia?

Who was it who said that for our sins there was all forgiveness, but our mistakes even infinite mercy could not pardon? Virginia was a mistake of his; that was all. It was safer to blame himself, not her—not her. That way lay madness.

Perhaps she, too, had found herself mistaken. Was that the secret he sometimes fancied he saw stirring behind the curtain of her placid eyes? If so, God pity them; and God help him to play the part he had to play.

He had reached his own threshold, and his latch-key faltered in the door. As he stepped into the wide hall, a curious figure in the disarray of his fastidious attire, he caught the odor of roses—they were Maréchal Niels—floating out of the drawing-room. The rooms were warm and bright and sweet, but their cheer seemed to him oppressive, and he sickened at the faint perfume of the roses.

His wife came and put the portière aside, standing with one white, lifted arm outlined against its heavy folds. Virginia always wore simple evening dress at home for her husband. She had been heard to say that it was one of the amenites that made domestic life endurable.

"How long you have been out!" she said, in just her usual sweet, unhurried voice, ignoring his dishevelled aspect. "I am afraid you are quite chilled through."

He looked at her an instant curiously— this exquisite piece of flesh and blood that was his second self for time and eternity— realizing that he did not understand her, had never understood her, could never hope nor desire to do so again. Then he gathered himself together to make the first speech in the part he had appointed hereafter to play— that rôle of devoted husband, whose cues he knew by heart. As he spoke he was shivering slightly, but surely that was because of the raw outer air.

"What a charming pose!" he said. "Did I ever tell you that throughout Homer 'white-armed' is used as a synonyme for beautiful?"

RIVALS

RIVALS

"I DIDN'T presume to suppose that you could care for me yet," said Rollinson, humbly.

"I am not at all sure that I cannot," said the girl, meditatively, "but, then, neither am I at all sure that I can." She looked at him with clear, untroubled eyes as she spoke, eyes in which he read her interest, her detachment, and her exquisite sincerity. She had not grown fluttered or self-conscious over his avowal. She was a modern woman, and she was young. Nothing had yet happened in her life to disturb her conviction that this was a subject upon which one could reason as upon other subjects. She was not emotional, and she suspected that the poets were not unerring guides in matters of the heart. She liked Rollinson very much, and she was willing to listen to his arguments.

It seemed to her a little strange that he did not proceed with those arguments at once, when suddenly she perceived that the adoration in his eyes was intended as the chief of them, and this discovery was so disconcerting that she blushed.

"I am twenty years older than you," murmured Rollinson. As this was the fact he most wished to forget, he felt it his duty to remind her of it.

"Nineteen only," she answered, calmly, "and, besides, I do not see what that has to do with it. It is not the years but the man one marries."

"It is very good of you to think so," he answered, still humbly, "and since there is no one else you care for, perhaps in time—"

He left the sentence hanging in the air, as if afraid to finish it, and neither this modesty nor the yearning tenderness of his accent was lost upon the girl.

"As you say, there is no one else."

"But—but there might be," suggested Rollinson, who was strongly possessed by the insane delusion of the lover that all men must needs worship his lady. "Bertha! If you are going to learn to love me, make haste to be kind. I am horribly unreasonable. I see a rival in every man you speak to, dance with, smile at. Until my probation is over

I should like to depopulate the world you move in. I want, at least, to be rejected on my own demerits, not because of the merits of another man!"

Bertha regarded him attentively, still with that serious, candid air.

"Indeed, I will try," she murmured, and for the moment he wisely said no more.

Rollinson had been a thoughtful youth, who early conceived of old age—which he thought began between forty and forty-five—as one of the most desirable periods of life.

"Patience! Afterwards," he had said to himself during the storm and stress, the confusion and uncertainty of youth — "afterwards, when I am old, when all this fermentation has ceased, when I know what I think, what I feel, what I want and can do, how glorious life will be!"

And in accordance with this conception, as he advanced in years, he looked confidently for the subsidence of the swelling tide of his prejudices, passions, partialities, and for the emergence of reason undefiled as the second Ararat upon which the long-tossed and buffeted ark of his mind might rest.

To say the least, he was taken aback when, in the midst of those ripe years, whose fruitage he had hoped to gather in great peace, he came again upon tempestuous days. In brief, when past forty, it befell him to love as he had never loved before, and with an unrest far exceeding that of youth, for he could not fail to see that the chances were by rights against him.

"Good Lord!" said Rollinson, when he faced his emotional condition, "for the heart there *is* no afterwards!"

But, happily, Bertha did not think so ill of his chances for happiness as did he himself, and he ventured to hope, although he was terrified by her calmness and her ability to see from all sides the subject he could only see from one.

Bertha respected his learning and revered his wisdom—which is learning hitched to life—and envied his experiences, and exulted in his grasp of people and things, and in his breadth of vision. She thought such a grip upon life as he possessed could only come with years. And compared to these things the disadvantages which also come with years seemed trifling. Obesity, baldness, and a touch of ancestral gout were the penalties he had to pay for being what he was. On the whole, the price did not seem too high. She felt quite sure that she would ultimately accept him, and that they would marry and live happily ever after.

This impression was still strong in her mind when, some days after the conversation recorded, she went with her aunt to a little lunch-party which he gave in his bachelor apartments.

Although he modestly spoke of them as being very simple, Rollinson's rooms were really a liberal education. He had been about the world a great deal and had carried with him fastidious taste and a purse only moderately filled. As he said once, he had never had so much money that he could afford to buy trash. The result was very happy. Pictures, rugs, draperies, brasses, ceramics, all were satisfactory.

"Your things are so delightfully intelligent!" said Bertha, with a gratified sigh. He found himself by her side as she was inspecting a bit of antique silver on a cabinet with obvious approval. "It makes me feel as I have never felt before, what a wonderful thing is taste!"

He smiled. "I am more than repaid if they have pleased you," he said. "Will you step this way an instant? I want to show you the thing I am vain enough to value most of all."

In the corner which he indicated, hung a picture she had not noticed, the portrait of a young man about twenty-five. The girl stared at it with fascinated eyes. "You! Can it be *you?*" she questioned, with an accent that was almost a reproach. Ah, how splendid he was, the painted youth in his hunter's costume who stood there fixed forever in all the beautiful insolence of his young manhood! What a mass of dark hair tossed back from his fine forehead, and what soldierly erectness in his bearing! How the eyes flashed — those eyes that only twinkled now! He was radiant, courageous, strong. What a hold he had on life — one read it in the lines of his mouth, in his eyes, his brow. What zest, what eagerness of spirit! He was more than all that she most admired in her lover, and he was young—young!

The girl gave a strange look at Rollinson and then turned back to the picture again. All fulfilment is pitiful compared with its prophecy, and in that moment she realized this.

"It was painted by my friend Van Anden, who died too early to achieve the fame he should have had," said Rollinson. "All that toggery I am wearing, which paints so effectively, was part of my outfit when I went to Africa with my cousin."

"It is very fine," said Bertha, with constraint, and then, with an unmistakably final movement, she turned away from it. Rollinson felt a sudden, wretched pang. If she cared at all for him, would not she also exult in this fair presentment of his young years?

After the luncheon had been served and before his guests had moved to go, he saw with a hopeful thrill that she had gone back to the picture and was standing before it again, intent and questioning.

He went up to her.

"Bertha! Dearest!" he said, beneath his breath. "After all, you like it, then?"

She turned upon him sharply. "It is wonderful—wonderful! But you should not have shown it to me! I do not understand. I—I thought I could have married you. Now I know that I never can. I—I never dreamed there was youth like that in the world. Oh, why did you let me find it out?"

Rollinson stood dumfounded.

"But it is I," he found voice to plead at

last. "Bertha, have the added years of worthy life made me less deserving of your love? Am I to be punished for becoming what he only promised to be?"

The girl passed her hand over her eyes in a bewildered way.

"It seems to me that one can love promise better than achievement," she said, faintly. "To care for what is not, is, I fancy, the very essence of love."

"I love you as he never could have done," urged Rollinson. "As he never dreamed of caring for any one. His loves were superficial and selfish, Bertha. I have gained much, and I have lost nothing that—that is essential."

"You have lost comprehension—he would have understood what I mean," answered the girl, quickly.

"But—Bertha! This is unreasonable. How can you expect me to comprehend?"

"I have been too reasonable!" she cried, with sudden passion. "That is my discovery. Love is not reasonable, youth is not—and they belong together. Oh, don't, don't make me say any more!"

For an instant there was a heavy silence

between them; then Rollinson found voice to say:

"It shall be as you please. Your aunt seems to be looking for you. Shall we go over to her?"

When his guests were gone at last, Rollinson came back to the picture. He took it down and placed it upon a chair where the light fell full upon it. Truly, he did not look like that to-day.

Although it was himself, he hated it, for it had cost him something dearer than the young strength which it portrayed. Of all the irrational humiliations of the long, wayward years of life this seemed to him the most hideous.

He took his knife from his pocket, opened it and put the point against the canvas. It would be easy to satisfy the brute anger in his soul by two sharp cross-cuts which should effectually destroy that remote, insolent beauty which had once been his own and now was his no longer.

He hesitated a moment, then dropped the knife and shook his head. He could not possibly do such a melodramatic, tawdry thing as that.

He knew that the day might yet come

when he should not remember the bitterness of this hour ; he might even grow to be glad again that he had once walked the earth in the likeness of this picture, but just now— just now he must forget it for awhile.

With one short sigh, Rollinson lifted the portrait of his rival and set it down, the face against the wall.

AT THE END OF THE WORLD

AT THE END OF THE WORLD

> " And so, as kinsmen met a night,
> We talked between the rooms,
> Until the moss had reached our lips,
> And covered up our names."

SHE was sitting quietly in the sleeper, writing a letter to a friend. She had got as far as "I feel it my duty to tell you," when the pencil flew out of her fingers. She had an instantaneous impression, grotesque in its horror, that all the natural laws were being unsettled with a terrible, grinding noise; for the pencil was falling toward the ceiling instead of the floor, and the man in front of her was following it, and even she herself. Then something struck her head and she lost consciousness.

When she came to herself she was lying on a cot in one corner of a large, unfamiliar room. As her gaze wandered slowly from object to object on the whitewashed walls, she concluded, from the combination of railway maps, time-cards, dusty windows filled with geraniums in pots, and a large, rusty Bible chained to a wall-pocket, that she was in a country railroad station; but when she turned her head she saw that it also resembled a hospital. She felt bruised and sore, but was not in much pain, and only an indefinable sensation of great weakness warned her not to move.

Presently some one noticed that her eyes were open and, drawing near, asked her some questions. She answered them with ease, and then in her turn asked a few. The man, obviously a physician, answered briefly but definitely. Then he drew a notebook from his pocket, took down some addresses that she gave him, and moved away softly in the direction of the telegraph window. She lay, looking after him incredulously. So this was death! She had at farthest two more hours on earth. It was part of her creed that one may permit one's self to be surprised but never startled. She was not startled now, but, decidedly, she was sorry. Her best work was yet undone, and she had not meant to leave earth while there still remained so much to do.

The sounds and sights of the hastily improvised hospital were unpleasant to her, and she turned her head away from them. There was one cot between her and the corner. She recognized the profile of that bandaged head as belonging to the man who had sat across the aisle in the sleeper. She had jotted down a description of him in her note-book, thinking she might use it some day. It ran:

"Sallow skin, soft, brown hair, fine eyes, but an iron mouth with a devil-may-care expression. He has the get-up of a man who is too busy being prosperous to take time to be comfortable. His face, a singular combination of sensitiveness and stolidity, the latter leading. Neither hard enough for this world nor tender enough for the next. An Achilles with a dozen vulnerable spots, he sheds two drops of his own blood for every one he draws in his battles; so, whether he wins or not, they are always losing fields for him."

She lay, looking at his profile, thinking that never, so long as she lived, could she see the other side of that anguished countenance, and the thought irritated her. This, she reflected, was an instance of the strength of the ruling passion. She had always been thirstily curious about life, even to its least details. Now the opportunities for quenching that thirst were at an end. There was no more for her in this world of that friction of spirit upon spirit which she loved. She was dying in a corner. Between herself and the immensity of eternity hung only that one white face.

Suddenly a thought came into her mind. Why should she not talk to him—while she was waiting?

"Are you badly hurt?" she asked, softly.

He groaned. "I am a dead man."

"They tell me I am dying, too," she said. "Why have they put us here in this corner, away from the others?"

"Because neither of us is in great pain, and we are both hopeless cases. They have no time to waste on us."

"It is very strange to think that this is really the last of it. Are you prepared to die?"

"Prepared? What is prepared?" he answered. "One is never ready to stop living. And there were a great many things I wanted to do yet."

"Were any of them important?"

An ironic smile twisted the corner of his

lips. "Now that you mention it—no. I wanted to make a good deal more money. I was going to turn over two or three pieces of real estate next week that I expected a profit upon. I meant to build a finer house for my wife—a big, new one, with all the modern wrinkles of architecture and furnishing. Then, if I had known she was going to have charge of things so soon, I should have altered one or two investments"——

His pain grew sharper and he groaned. When he was still she spoke again.

"If I had met you yesterday I should have said that your interests in life were very much less fine and spiritual than my own. I wrote things that people praised. They said I was clever, ingenious, witty; but they never said I was an artist. I meant to make them say it. I was going to write a novel next winter that should show"— She stopped, but presently went on, musingly: "It is very odd, but somehow it doesn't seem as important as it did this morning. Do you care that your house will never be built?"

"No."

"And I don't care about my novel. I called my interest in life art, and you called yours business; but neither of them seems to count any more. The question is, What does count?"

"Close your eyes and lie still for five minutes, and note what you find yourself unable to avoid thinking of. That will show you what counts."

"You have been trying it?"

He made a motion of assent.

"Well," he asked, after a silence on her part that seemed long, "does it work?"

"Yes," she said, in a tense way; "it works too well. What did *you* see?"

Again the ironic smile twisted the visible corner of his mouth. "Shall we exchange confidences—last confessions, and all that? I'd just as soon. Reticence isn't worth much now. Only—you begin."

"I saw," she said, slowly, "my husband's eyes. I had forgotten how they looked when he found that I really meant to insist on a separation. He could not bear it, for he adored the ground I walked on. It was five years ago. I had no presentable reason for leaving him. He was so horribly good-natured that it used to irritate me. And I didn't care for the domestic life. It interfered with my work, although he had promised that it should not. I wanted to be free again. He let me have the child. He was very good about the whole business—painfully good, in fact. But it did hurt him cruelly. I have been very much happier since, but I don't suppose he has."

"Did he have brown eyes—the big, faithful, dog-like kind?" asked the man.

"How did you know?"

"That good sort often do. The girl I jilted did. We had been engaged almost from our cradles. There was an accident with horses, and she got hurt. She limped a little afterward, and there were scars on her face and neck—not very bad scars, but still they were there. She had been a little beauty before that; but she never at any time thought much about her looks, and it hadn't occurred to her that I minded. But I did mind. I fretted over it until I fancied that I didn't love her, after all; but I did. One day I told her so. You know how she looked at me. She asked if the accident made any difference, and I hadn't the skill to lie about it so that she believed me. She rose at once, as if to put an end to our interview. All she said was, 'I thought you knew better what love was.' I can hear how her voice sounded. She was badly cut up; lost her health and all that. And I never could pretend I wasn't to blame. The girl I married later was faultlessly pretty, but there was nothing in the world to her."

"We seem to be a nice sort, don't we?" said the woman, reflectively.

"We are no worse than others. Unselfishness is out of fashion. Everybody takes what he wants nowadays."

"My husband didn't."

"I respect your husband. But you did it. We did the same sort of thing, you and I; only I think you are the worse of the two. It is natural for a man to want a wife who isn't disfigured."

"It is natural for a clever woman to want to live unfettered."

"Perhaps. But I erred through the worser part of my nature, and you through the better. My revolt against unselfishness was physical, and yours intellectual. Therefore you fell farther than I, by as much as the mind is better than the body; don't you see?"

"That is speciously put, but I doubt its truth."

Both were silent for a space.

"I have it!" she breathed suddenly, and her voice was stronger; for even in the clutches of death a new insight into the meaning of things had power to stimulate her whole being. "It is this way. Our error was the same. We both betrayed their trust in us. We grieved love. And the reason that we remember now is that love and God are one, and this is the judgment. That is why we see their eyes rebuking us. It comes to us, now that we die. That is all life is for—to learn not to grieve love. Why did I never know it before? Oh, if I had put that in my books!"

"If you had put it in your life it would have been better," interrupted the man; but she went on, unheeding:

"That must be what they meant when they said my work lacked conviction. It is the heart that takes sides. One man said I was too clever to be interesting. I never understood what he meant before, but I see now. It was that I had mind enough but too little heart. I wanted to become as one of the gods by knowing, and the appointed path is by loving. To be human and to love is to be divine."

"Oh, wise conclusion!" mocked the man.

"What does it profit you to know it — now?"

She was silent, spent with the effort of her eager speech. The maps on the opposite wall whirled before her eyes. She felt herself slipping — slipping. Yet, though she found no words to tell him why, there came to her a sudden, sweet assurance that it profited her much, even at this last hour, to know the thing she had just spoken.

It was a long time before she found strength to ask: "Shall you be here after I am gone?"

"Why?"

"I gave them my husband's name. I knew he would be glad to come. He lives a hundred miles from here, and it will only take him four hours at the longest. I shall not last that long. If you would tell him" —

"Tell him what?"

"Tell him," said the woman, slowly, "that I saw; that I am sorry I grieved love and him; that I wish I had been wiser about what life meant; that love is always best."

"The fact is," said the man, reluctantly, "I did not mean to stay. I dabbled in medicine a little once, and I know that I can last this way a day or two. But I am in pain now, and it will grow worse. What is the use of staying? They tied an artery for me; it might easily get untied, you know."

"Aren't you going to wait until your wife comes?" she asked, wonderingly.

"Better not," answered the man, briefly. "It would hurt her less this way, and me too. Scenes worry me, and her nerves are delicate"

"What farces such marriages as yours are!"

"Better a farce than a tragedy. My wife has been happier than your husband. She has been very comfortable, and she will continue to be so, for my estate is reasonably large."

"Then Arthur will never know that I am sorry, and I want him to. Oh, God! I want him to."

The man lay, frowning sharply at the ceiling. The ineffectual anguish of her cry had touched him, but his pain was growing worse. At last he spoke.

"Look here. If I will stay and deliver that message for you, will you do something for me?"

"I? What can I do for any one?"

"You are a woman, though not, it seems, a very loving one. You can tell me if there is any forgiveness for the hurt I gave that girl, and if there is, absolve me in love's name! I cannot bear her eyes."

"Love forgives everything," she answered, simply. "Wait until you see Arthur's face when you tell him I was sorry. That will show you."

"Say it!" murmured the man, peremptorily. "Let me hear the words, as she might say them."

She turned upon her side to smile at him. Her voice had grown so faint that it seemed but a disembodied, yearning tenderness that spoke.

"In love's name, then, and hers, *absolvo te*"— And the thread of sound dropped into a silence that was to remain unbroken.

The man lay still, clenching his hands and unclenching them. The thrusts of pain had grown very sharp, but he grimly set his teeth. He might ask for morphine; but if he took it "Arthur" might come and go while he lay in stupor, and the message remain forever undelivered. He looked at the clock on the opposite wall. Perhaps he had still three hours to wait. What should he do? That last dart was keenest of them all. What did people do in torture, people who had made promises that they must stay to keep? Surely there was something. Ah, that was it. Of course. They prayed. Then why not he, as well?

His lips moved feverishly.

"Christ, thou who suffered for love's sake, give me—give me the pluck to hold out three hours more."

www.ingramcontent.com/pod-product-compliance
Lightning Source LLC
Chambersburg PA
CBHW020245170426
43202CB00008B/234